Career Education: A Priority of the Chief State School Officers

DAVID L. JESSER
Council of Chief State School Officers

Olympus Publishing Company Salt Lake City, Utah

Library of Congress Cataloging in Publication Data

Jesser, David L.
    Career education.

    Bibliography: p.
    Includes index.
    1.   Vocational education—United States.
2.   Vocational guidance—United States.   I.   Title
LC1044.J47   370.11'3   74-29667
ISBN 0-913420-46-8

Contents

List of Figures

Foreword

Within the system of education that prevails in the United States, the primary and fundamental responsibility for public education rests with the individual states; and within each state, a state education agency, headed by a chief state school officer, is responsible for the administration, supervision, and general operation of the educational program in the state. The degree to which the state education agencies have been able to assume their responsibilities is due in large measure to the leadership and vision that has been demonstrated by the chief state school officers. It is the chief state school officer who has the ultimate responsibility for leadership of the educational program in his or her state — an educational program which encompasses all of public education, spanning general and vocational, and which includes all potential learners as clients.

In seeking to meet their leadership responsibilities, the chief state school officers — through their professional organization, the Council of Chief State School Officers — have consistently indicated both a willingness to explore and a desire to test ideas that might potentially benefit or improve upon the existing educational program. Such a commitment has been made by the Council of Chief State School Officers relative to career education.

When the concept of career education was first advanced in 1971 by Sidney P. Marland, at that time Commissioner of Education in the U.S. Office of Education, many leaders and educational organizations seemed to agree with the concept, at least in principle. The Council of Chief State School Officers, comprised of the educational leaders charged with the responsibility for the educational programs in each state, not only agreed with the concept, but has gone on record as strongly supporting career education as a means of more adequately meeting the educational — and life — needs of learners.

The Council, however, recognizes that in American education there have been many educational innovations that have appeared upon and then disappeared from the educational scene. Some have disappeared because of misinformation, unrealistic expectations, or sheer impracticability. Others have disappeared because adequate foundational efforts were not made before implementation was attemped. Still others have vanished because they did not mesh with existing value systems, goal statements, or educational priorities. And of course there have been educational innovations which have had a high degree of emotional appeal — popular appeal — and which have caused large numbers to "get on the bandwagon."

Cognizant as it was of the caveats concerning educational innovations, yet highly supportive of the concept of career education, the Council initiated procedures that would (a) adequately account for the several caveats and (b) encourage and enhance the solid implementation of career education. A major step in this direction was the preparation, submission, and subsequent approval of a proposal to the U.S. Office of Education for a study to be conducted of career education.

The study, funded for a twelve-month period by USOE, started in the spring of 1973 and ended in May 1974. It was designed to enable the chief state school officers and their respective state education agencies to have ready access to information about career education: what it is, how it might operate, what its goals and purposes are, and the like. In addition, it was hoped that the project would also provide chief state school officers and state education agencies with models, alternatives, and guidelines that would be of value to them in their efforts to implement or expand career education programs. Specifically, it was intended that the project would review and make recommendations concerning:

(1) The concepts of career education

(2) Identification of appropriate elements of career education

(3) Development and adaptation of curriculum materials for career education

(4) Methods of state-level organization and leadership of career education programs

With both the broad goals and specific purposes in mind, personnel in the project throughout its duration gathered, assembled, synthesized, and disseminated information as it relates to career education.

The information — which was used in the preparation of project materials — was gathered in a variety of ways and from a variety of sources. For example, information relating to the concept of career education was obtained mainly from professional literature and state plans or statements. Information about state-level organization, on the other hand, was gathered largely through questionnaires (see chapter 1 for results) or personal contacts and on-site visits. The project also produced a fairly comprehensive collection of documents relating to career education operations in several states. (This has also served as an excellent source of information about various models and alternatives.) Finally, a most important source of information was found to be state directors (or coordinators) of career education in each of the participating states. Because of the information that was assembled and of the assistance given by personnel in the state education agencies, it was possible for those working in the project to engage in a series of pertinent activities, to produce a series of reports, and to participate in and sponsor leadership efforts in career education. (Subsequently, a conference — reported later in the book — was held in Dallas, Texas, on April 29 and 30 and May 1, 1974; the degree of response is indicated by the representation at the conference: 43 states and three territories.)

As for the reports — five papers were written and were then compiled into a final report to USOE. These now become chapters 1 through 5 of this book. The original study, titled "Career Education in Public Education: Mission, Goals, and Methods," can be obtained from the ERIC Clearinghouse in Career Education (CE 002 152-002-158). This book, it is hoped, will benefit not only advocates and practitioners of but also neophytes in career education.

In the original report, each paper carried its own preface; but because some of these were identical, the prefaces are printed here.

Preface to Chapter 1

The education system that exists in the United States in the mid-1970s has often been described as a system in which nineteenth century methods and concepts are being used to help twentieth century youngsters learn to cope with life as it will exist in the latter years of the twentieth century and in the first third of the twenty-first century. For some educators and lay citizens, such a characterization may be inaccurate and hence unworthy of consideration. But for others, the characterization seems to portray, with painful accuracy, the current scene in American education.

Educational leaders who perceive even an element of truth in the above description have exhibited deep concern about the educational program and have raised serious questions. While doing so, they have been, and are, engaged in various endeavors and activities in their search for plausible and possible solutions.

Concerns, questions, and activities such as these have been, over the years, largely responsible for many of the major changes that have occurred in American education. Indeed, similar concern, study, and action will undoubtedly continue to be the hallmarks for major changes in the education system in future years.

At the present time, as a result of the voicing of serious concern about the relationship of the education system to the world of work, questions are again being raised, and attempts are being made to find ways of achieving a long-honored, but often ignored, educational goal: helping students become useful, contributing, and productive members of the society in which they will live. As one consequence of these efforts, it is becoming evident that a new role — or at least a new emphasis — will be identified or defined for American education. In the new role that is beginning to emerge, it is evident that the education system will in all likelihood address itself in more direct fashion than ever before to ways of *helping individuals prepare for total life careers*, as opposed to preparing them for *specific occupations only* or for *further education only*. The education system, as it assumes its new role, will have as its primary focus the total career process of every individual — a process that extends from an individual's early childhood years through the mature adult retirement years.

The emerging redefinition of the role or purpose of education, as indicated above, has resulted in the development and wide acceptance of a new and promising concept: career education. By effectively using this concept, educators might possibly narrow the gap — which some say exists in the education system — between the nineteenth and twenty-first centuries. In any event, proper and carefully considered use of the concept should result in the creation of a more meaningful learning environment for all.

Preface to Chapter 2

The Roman philosopher, Seneca, is supposed to have observed that unless you know what port you are sailing to, the direction of the wind makes little difference. This observation, it would seem, has considerable relevance for educators who are conscientiously attempting to transform the concept of career education into a viable educational process. Unless the goals of career education are clear — understood and accepted by those concerned — the process that is initiated is likely to be of little consequence in the final analysis.

In the preceding paper of this series [chapter 1] mention was made of the fact that from the many innovations in education that have been introduced, few have really been actually incorporated into the education system. The lack of clarity of purpose or goals may well have been a contributing factor. Perhaps as has been suggested in a recent publication of the United States Chamber of Commerce, innovative educators, in their haste to arrive at the solution to a problem, have indeed been prone to "jump right over the problem and into the solution." In other words, they may have neglected to ascertain what it was they wanted to accomplish.

As efforts to expand the use of the concept of career education continue, care must be exercised by educational leaders to ensure that the goals – the overriding purposes – do not become faded, dim, or unrecognizable.

Goals and purposes are, of necessity and by definition, broad in scope. They attempt to provide answers to questions such as:

(1) What do we want our children to become?

(2) What do we want children to value?

(3) How do we want children to behave?

(4) What do we want children to know about themselves and the world about them?

(5) What do we want children to be able to feel, touch, smell, see, and hear?

(6) What abilities do we want children to develop?

(7) What tasks should children be able to perform?

(8) What should children know about deriving pleasure? About freedom? About responsibility?

(9) What should children know about making choices and selecting alternatives? And how can they learn to deal constructively with the constant fact of change?

It should be emphasized that while goals may differ somewhat, or may be phrased in different ways, they are more likely to be similar than different – assuming that they are well thought out and commonly accepted.

Some of the purposes and goals of career education are examined and discussed in chapter 2. Educators who have responsibility for the development and implementation of career education may choose to add others or to modify those that are discussed. Irrespective of the goals that are defined, however, they should reflect the basic purposes of the endeavor.

And at the same time, it is imperative that they also reflect the idea that career education, as it is perceived, is a means to an end — not an end in and of itself.

Preface to Chapters 3 and 4

As pointed out in the preface to chapter 2 of this series, people should know where they want to go before they set out on a journey. Stated in more explicit fashion, they should know what they want to do or accomplish before they begin the task.

In much the same vein, it is necessary for people, as they identify goals and purposes, to have some idea of the options that are open to them. For example, when one considers travel from one place to another, numerous options are available and should be carefully considered before one decides on the route to be taken, the mode of travel, and perhaps the time frame to be used.

So it is with career education efforts: When a determination of purpose has been made and agreed upon, those responsible for implementation will need to consider the many options that are open to them, of materials that might be employed, target populations, and the like.

To be sure, those responsible for implementation of career education programs will obviously have to consider the options in light of varying conditions, constraints, and restraints that might exist in a given community. But this in no way negates the need to know the options that exist and how each might facilitate installation or expansion of career education efforts.

Chapters 3 and 4 of this series, having to do with materials and models respectively, are intended to be of assistance to state education agency personnel as they continue in their efforts to make career education a reality in their states.

Preface to Chapter 5

In the preceding four chapters of this series, an attempt has been made to gather together, synthesize, and disseminate information relating to career education. Chapter 1 traced the evolution and development of the career education concept and pointed out the various ways in which it has been defined.

It also implied a need for some common frame of reference for career education among state education agencies and presented several broad issues which should be seriously considered by those agencies as they continue to implement the concept.

In chapter 2, the various reasons why career education appears to hold significant potential for needed reforms in education were presented. Implicit in chapter 2 is the caution that as state education agencies either plan or implement career education programs, they should carefully examine and perhaps redefine or modify the purposes that have been given to ensure that the goals – the expected outcomes – are clear.

As was implied in chapter 3, specifically designed tools are needed for certain tasks. In this vein, various "tools" (i.e., curricular materials) that have been developed for use in the implementation of career education efforts were presented. In addition, some of the criteria for such tools and materials were also discussed.

In chapter 4, the necessary components of career education, as it has been treated in the series, were discussed, as were the several characteristics which appear to be common to most career education programs or definitions. In addition, representative models or schemata that have been developed and used by state education agencies were included.

In this paper, the role of the state education agency, as it relates to career education, is discussed, as are several strategies that might be used. Finally, from the information gathered and disseminated, several implications for state education agencies seem apparent. These are also discussed.

Collectively, the papers in this series should serve as a valuable resource and reference as well as a source of ideas for chief state school officers and their staffs as they continue to translate career education from a concept to a functional and operational reality.

Conclusion

The preface to chapter 1 was written by Byron W. Hansford, Executive Secretary of the Council of Chief State School Officers. Those for chapters 2 through 4 were written by David L. Jesser, Director of this project. And last but not least, chapter 5 was prefaced by William I. Israel, Director of Special Projects, Council of Chief State School Officers.

The Council is appreciative of having had the opportunity to actively participate in the study. It has been informative and useful. Much information has been gathered and distributed to chief state school officers and to their staffs. Many alternative methods, models, and definitions have been presented as a result of other project efforts; it has been possible to ascertain that much has already been accomplished. At the same time, there still remains much to be done before career education will truly be part of the total education system. More information will have to be gathered; more "risk capital" will have to be made available; teacher preparation programs will have to be changed. These are but a few tasks which remain. It is the hope of the Council that in a continuation of the current effort, the necessary tasks can be undertaken.

We also wish to acknowledge the valuable assistance and support that has been provided by the Council of Chief State School Officers and its Committee on Career Education, headed by Cecil E. Stanley, Commissioner of Education for Nebraska. At the same time, we want to express our appreciation to Kenneth B. Hoyt, Sidney High, Gerald Elbers and Elizabeth Simpson, all of the U.S. Office of Education, for their assistance and support.

David L. Jesser
Project Director

1

The
Concept
of Career
Education

David L. Jesser

From time to time throughout the history of educational thought and development in the United States, concerns and doubts have been raised about various aspects of the education system. As a result, many suggestions and recommendations concerning ways in which the perceived inadequacies, inequities, and deficiencies might be remedied have been made. Some have resulted in lasting and significant changes in the system. The high school, the industrial arts curriculum, and vocational education programs are but a few examples of lasting and significant changes that have been effected as a result of serious and overriding concerns relating to perceived inadequacies of the educational program.

On the other hand, the literature is replete with examples of suggestions and recommendations for change that were offered (and in some instances implemented on a somewhat limited and localized basis) but had little or no lasting impact on American education. New or different curricular approaches have been suggested and developed; new and different organizational patterns have been created; new and different administrative arrangements have been attempted; and new and different architectural settings have been designed and built. These are some examples of changes that have been suggested but which have not had the impact desired by those who propose them.

Of all the suggestions and recommendations that have been made relating to desired changes in the American education system, however, few have been met with such instant acceptance as has the concept of career education. As is noted in a subsequent section, there are those who would assert that the concept in various forms has existed for a long while. But it was not until early in 1971 that it was introduced as a single and recognizable suggestion for a major change in the education system. Sidney P. Marland, the U.S. Commissioner of Education in the U.S. Department of Health, Education, and Welfare (HEW), presented the suggestion — together with the concept — to members of the National Association of Secondary School Principals who were meeting in Houston in January 1971. In the relatively short time since its introduction, the concept has burgeoned, with an almost supernova-like quality, across the nation and has had immense impact on every educational level with a vigor seldom witnessed in education in the United States. The manner in which it has been received has suggested that career education is a concept "whose time had come" (Hoyt *et al.*, 1974, p. 11).

The rapidity with which the concept of career education has been accepted, together with the almost messianic fervor with which many educational leaders have embraced it, is no doubt a reflection of innumerable concerns and doubts about the validity of the roles and functions of education and educators, together with concerns and doubts relating to the reliability with which the education system is performing its perceived roles and functions. In a more global sense, the rapidity of acceptance is perhaps a reflection of a basic concern about societally based problems which are becoming increasingly evident in the United States during the waning years of the twentieth century. Concerns about the education system, together with concerns about broad-based societal problems, have again caused educators and concerned citizens to search for "better ways." And they seem to perceive career education as a way to help:

(1) The forty million elementary school children who need career orientation

(2) The 7.5 million young people who seek employment after graduation

(3) The unemployed, or soon to be unemployed, workers not expecting callback because of shifts in technology or shifts in labor market demand

(4) The highly motivated working poor stuck in low-skill, low-paying jobs, who need to hold two jobs to earn enough to cover their family needs

(5) The mothers of school-age children who need and want to reenter the labor market

(6) Older workers, involuntarily retired, who want to continue to work but need a marketable skill

(7) The more than three hundred thousand mental hospital patients discharged every year who need a marketable skill to sustain themselves

(8) The inmates in our prisons who need pre- and post-release skills training to cut down on the high rate of recidivism

(9) The more than three million children and youth considered to be learning handicapped, who are prime candidates for special training programs that will provide them with the economic or psychological means to be fulfilled individuals

For many concerned educators, legislators, parents, and taxpayers, career education holds the promise and the potential of greatly helping society cope with the problems of the many individuals alluded to above. At the same time, and more important, they see in career education a means of helping the individual to be better equipped to aggressively resolve, as well as to cope with, the many problems of society.

What Is Career Education?

It has been suggested that career education, at least at the present time, might best be described as a concept in search of a definition. This observation, it should be noted, may not be completely accurate in a literal sense because, as has been observed, there are perhaps as many definitions of career education as there are people who are trying to develop or implement programs. But as the observation implies, there is an apparent lack of unanimity concerning the definition, if not the meaning, of career education.

It should be recognized by all concerned that there is a genuine need for at least a broad definition of career education that would establish a perceptual framework or parameter in which educators might be able to function, but which at the same time would provide the freedom for needed adaptation. As pointed out in a later section, many such broad definitions of career education have been developed by state education agencies. An example that would be of value in the context of the immediate discussion, however, is a definition that has been developed by the Task Force on Career Education of the Council of Chief State School Officers (ccsso):

> Career education is essentially an instructional strategy, aimed at improving educational outcomes by relating teaching and learning activities to the concept of career development. Career education extends the academic world to the world of work. In scope, career education encompasses educational experiences beginning with early childhood and continuing throughout the individual's productive life. A complete program of career education includes awareness of the world of work, broad orientation to occupations (professional and nonprofessional), in-depth exploration of selected clusters, career preparation, an understanding of the economic system of which jobs are a part, and placement for all students.

While the preceding definition (or a similar one) will be adequate for many, it should be recognized that for some educators and lay citizens, loose or broad definitions do not suffice. There are those who prefer — if not actually require — a recipe or somewhat definitive prepackaged program of career education. There is need for clear meaning; yet there is risk inherent in any kind of rigid prescription. No doubt this is what Dr. Marland had in mind when he indicated that "developing such a constraining definition would be the best way to kill the whole idea" (1972, p. 9).

While there are those (Marland, for example) who would see a positive value in having no single definition or "official" designation, it is interesting to note that numerous references in the literature contain definitions which have been developed. Hoyt *et al.* (1974) implied that a lack of definition of career education existed when they suggested that it was a "concept in search of a definition." They then went on to offer a definition:

> Career education is the total effort of public education and the community to help all individuals become familiar with the values of a work-oriented society, to integrate these values into their personal value systems, and to implement these values into their lives in such a way that work becomes possible, meaningful, and satisfying to each individual (pp. 15 and 100).

In similar fashion, while Marland indicated explicitly that career education should not be defined or prescribed in Washington, he offered some advice that suggested that career education should *not* be perceived as:

(1) A renaming of vocational-technical education

(2) An anti-intellectual conspiracy

(3) A way to discourage poor and minority young people from going to college

(4) Being limited to elementary and secondary schools

(5) Simply a means of getting a job

In a more positive vein, Marland (1972) suggested that career education is or should be perceived as:

> ...the companion to academic preparation at every grade level, from kindergarten through graduate school, so as to enable every young person to enter and do well in a career carefully chosen from among many, no matter at what point he or she leaves formal education (p. 19).

As Dr. Marland has described career education, it is clear that his hopes for its use extended far beyond what is now considered to be the scope of "formal education." To him, career education "offers the same opportunities to adults who reenter the system either to upgrade their competencies in a field of work or to leave their field" (pp. 19-20).

Both Hoyt and Marland attempted to give some meaning to the concept of career education and, at the same time, attempted to avoid a rigid set of rules or prescriptions. In similar fashion, other educators — from every type of educational structure — have developed fairly broad and comprehensive definitions.

As the emergent definitions or descriptions of career education are examined, the contributions of educators, sociologists, economists, and educational psychologists should not be overlooked. Some of these contributions have already been noted in those of Hoyt and his colleagues. Taken individually, these statements should serve as excellent guidelines:

> The fundamental concept of career education is that all types of educational experiences, curriculum, instruction, and counseling, should involve preparation for economic independence, personal fulfillment, and an appreciation for the dignity of work. It seeks to give meaning to all education by relating its content to the job world (p. 2).... Career education is not something which precedes participating in society but is an integration of learning and doing that merges the worlds of the home, the community, the school, and the workplace into a challenging and productive whole (p. 3).

In "Position Paper on Career Development," presented to the 1973 APGA convention in New Orleans, Tennyson and his associates sought to distinguish *career* from *occupation*:

> Sociologists and some psychologists have used the term "career" to refer to the sequence of occupations, jobs, and positions occupied during the course of a person's life. This definition is helpful in carrying the impost of developmental movement through structures, but it conveys no sense of an active person interacting with his environment....The term "career" means a time-extended working out of a purposeful life pattern through work undertaken and engaged in by the individual. Career can easily be differentiated from the term "career development," which refers to the total constellation of psychological, sociological, educational, physical, economic, and chance factors that combine to shape the career of any given indi-

vidual....The meaning of the word "career," then, is directly dependent upon the meaning one attaches to the word "work." Work, as conceived for purposes of this paper, may be defined as an expenditure of effort designed to effect some change, however slightly, in some province of civilization. It is not simply an arbitrary or gratuitous action, but something which, from some viewpoint within society, *ought* to be done. The concept carries the intention that an act of human effort will lead to an improvement of one's own condition or that of some element of society....Viewed in this way, work is not directly attached to paid employment, but it may include also efforts of an educational or avocational nature. Thus education for work and certain elements of leisure which are undertaken to benefit society or which contribute to a sense of individual purpose and achievement are included in this definition.

Tennyson *et al.* have provided the concerned educator with a framework in which programs of career development can be facilitated. In addition, they have provided a perspective which could serve to alleviate concerns that have been voiced by educationists, vocational education specialists, and vocational guidance personnel about who should have responsibility for what:

> ...It must be emphasized that a person's career does not unfold independently of other areas of his development. *Ultimately the educator, whatever his title, must concern himself with the total developing person*, and this implies a consideration of how work and career meshes with other life pursuits in a reasoned style of living. (Emphasis added.)

As has already been indicated, definitions such as these were developed primarily to provide guidelines — or broad directions — to those who might develop and implement programs in career education. They were not definitive; they were not intended to be. Yet they (together with many others not cited) performed the intended function well.

When the "broad strokes" that made up the guideline types of definition are used, more operational types of definitions are seen to evolve wherever serious attempts have been made to develop and implement career education programs. Such definitions have been developed by many state education agencies and include key concepts such as those below (see Selected References at end of chapter).

Arizona (1973, p. 5):

> A complete program of career education includes awareness of the world of work, broad exploration of occupations, in-depth exploration of selected clusters, and career preparation for all students.

Louisiana (Michot, 1973, p. 5):

> It is our responsibility as the adults of our society to provide the best education that Louisiana's resources permit, and it is the responsibility of our students to see that they avail themselves of every opportunity of discovering, deciding, and developing their life cycles and styles.

Nevada (1973, p. 11):

> Career education not only provides job information and skill development, but also aids students in developing attitudes about the personal, psychological, social, and economic significance of work.

New Mexico (1973, p. 1):

> Career education is essentially a lifelong process, beginning early in the preschool years and continuing, for most individuals, through retirement. As a process, it includes the view one has of himself and the possible work opportunities, the choices he makes related to himself as a worker, and the ways in which he implements those choices.

Ohio (1972, p. vi):

> Career education is defined as a program which endeavors, through the regular curriculum, to provide all youth in the school motivation toward the world of work, orientation to the many job opportunities available, and exploration of occupations consistent with individual interests and abilities.

Oregon (Kunzman, 1970):

> Schools have a threefold objective: to help young people (a) discover their individual interests and abilities, (b) explore the many avenues of productive activity that might challenge and enlarge their individual talents, and (c) learn the wise exercise of freedom of choice, self-direction, self-discipline, and responsibility.

Utah (1973, p. 6):

> Career education extends beyond the school and uses the entire community as a resource for career development. In this context, career education is not separate and apart from total life education, but is a correlated, integral part of all human development.

The preceding concepts of career education that have been developed in the various state education agencies are by no means intended as an exhaustive list. Obviously, there are many others that might have been identified and cited. But while the listing may not be all-inclusive, it is sufficiently representative to suggest that irrespective of specific terms or local adaptations, the concept of career education is made up of several basic characteristics:

(1) In scope, career education encompasses educational experiences beginning with early childhood and continuing through the individual's productive life.

(2) In early childhood, career education provides an awareness of self in relationship with the world of work, as well as direct experiences to motivate and captivate the learner's interest in the basic skills being taught.

(3) As children move through school, they increase their familiarity with the world of work and acquire knowledge necessary to obtain meaningful employment after leaving school.

(4) Career education also makes the provision to prepare individuals for employment and, later in their career, to upgrade their skills, to update their knowledge, and to retrain them for a new job if they wish it.

(5) Career education combines the academic world with the world of work. It must be available at all levels of education, from kindergarten through the university. A complete program of career education includes self-awareness of the world of work, broad exploration of selected work clusters, and career preparation for all students. This calls for all basic education subjects to incorporate career education as activity, motivation, and methodology.

As has been emphasized, there are many variations in the numerous definitions that have been developed for career education. So also is there variation in graphic portrayals that have been developed to depict the scope and character of career education. A fairly representative portrayal (Figure 1.1), however, has been developed by the Oregon State Department of Education, in which several elements of characteristics are shown. The schematic indicates where in the educational spectrum the several types of career education should ideally take

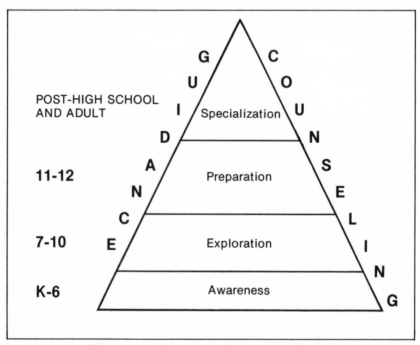

Figure 1.1. Oregon's Conceptual Model
of Career Education

place. It does not, however, attempt to portray how the programs or activities relate to the "total world." This type of relationship — i.e., that between career education and the "world" — is graphically portrayed in Figure 1.2. This model was developed by the Nevada state education agency.

Throughout this section considerable attention has been given to the numerous definitions, schemata, and models that have been developed to describe career education. A clear understanding of these is essential if career education is to have the thrust or impact that has been envisaged for it. But at the same time proponents and advocates of career education should not attempt to develop every notion or idea from a zero point. Career education is a new concept in American education; its roots, however, go back a long way.

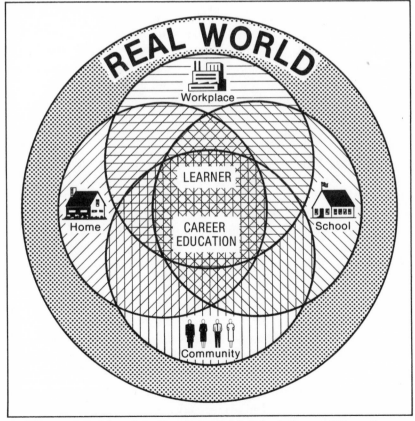

Figure 1.2. Nevada's Conceptual Model of Career Education

Evolution of the Concept of Career Education

To identify, with any degree of accuracy, all of the origins and antecedents of the concept of career education would be extremely difficult and time consuming, if not completely impossible. At the same time, such a descriptive account would not serve any really useful purpose in the context of this book. On the other hand, it is important that those responsible for planning, developing, and implementing programs of career education recognize that the concept did have clear and definable antecedents; that the concept did not "happen" in some spontaneous fashion.

According to Herr (1972, p. 3), career education in its current context should be recognized as

> ...a synthesis and blend of many concepts and elements available at some point and in some place in American education. However, the intent and implementation tactics so far apparent are to bring these concepts and elements into a new and systematic interrelationship among vocational education, vocational guidance, career development, and other elements of the educational and community networks of which they are part.

As Herr implies, some of the more prominent roots of career education are to be found in vocational education and vocational guidance programs. However, to say that in these programs are to be found the embryonic stages of career education would be erroneous, for the emphasis on and development of vocational programs are in reality a part of the evolutionary process that has now culminated in the emergence of career education.

Vocational education and vocational guidance have both had impact on the evolution of career education, but they have been supplemented by many other educational endeavors and "outside" influences. Many bases for career education existed before development of the concept of either vocational education or career education. Gordon Swanson reiterated this when he recently observed that career education, in various shapes and forms, has made partial and tentative appearances in

American education for more than a hundred years. Tyler (1973, p. 165), in a similar observation, notes:

> Although schools [of the 1820s] were seen as places where workers' children could learn a craft, [workers] consistently refused to limit schooling to what we today call "vocational education." They wanted their children to be more than skilled artisans; they also wanted them to be informed citizens.

Tyler, Herr, and others have traced the development of the concept of career education in some detail. For the educator or lay citizen who is interested in examining the antecedents of career education, the cited sources are highly recommended. For the purposes of this book, a summary of the historical, philosophical, and conceptual antecedents of career education, as prepared by Professor Herr (1972, pp. 29-30), should suffice:

> Virtually every concept which is presently embodied in career education has been advocated at some point in American education. This is not to suggest that such concepts have either been operationalized [sic] or tested in practice. Nevertheless, philosophical support for the major elements of career education has historical construct, if not evaluative validity.... Although there were antecedents in life adjustment and progressive education positions prior to 1960, increased emphasis has been focused on the prevocational elements of decision making and preparation to be found in the elementary, middle, or junior high school educational level. Equally important has been concern for the vocational implications held by post-secondary education, including collegiate education, for adults and out-of-school youth. Together these elements have constituted support for articulating, from kindergarten through post-secondary education, a series of increasingly complex educational experiences which would be available to all students, to out-of-school youth, and to adults. Further, these experiences are seen as requiring not only vocational preparation, but a continuum oriented to prevocational and educational awareness, attitudinal development, awareness of personal strengths and potentiali-

ties, as well as the development of decision-making abilities.

As has been observed, it is possible to identify many antecedents of career education, some of which may even pre-date the founding of the nation. All have contributed to the development of the concept. But, as indicated by Herr, it was not until the decade of the '60s that major attention was devoted to societal problems, inadequacies of education, and possible solutions. Attention of this nature was demonstrated in 1962 by the Panel of Consultants on Vocational Education (1963, p. 3) with the following statement:

> Of every ten students now enrolled in the elementary grades, three will probably not attain high school graduation. How will these three earn a living in the world of the 1960s without a high school diploma? How can the schools help them before and after they "drop out"? Of the other seven boys and girls who will finish high school in this decade, three will not go on to college. What will these three high school graduates do for a living? How well will their high school education prepare them to earn a living or, in the case of many girls, to perform the duties of housewife and mother? Of the remaining four students who will eventually enter college, only two will receive baccalaureate degrees. What are the prospects of the two who do not complete four years of college? How will high school and post-high school study help them earn a living?...Thus eight out of ten youngsters now in the elementary schools who have a need for vocational education are a major concern of this report. These young people will enter the labor force in this decade 26 million strong, and will account for nearly 90 percent of the growth in the labor force during the 1960s. By the end of the decade, three million young workers will enter the labor force each year, compared with two million annually at the start of the decade. Will these young workers be well prepared for the world of work? Will their interests, skills, and knowledge match the changing requirements of the economy?

The apparent appropriateness of the above concerns to the present-day situation, when contrasted to the time at which they were formulated (1962), might suggest to some that the concerns have had little or no impact. Any such perception, however, would be erroneous, for out of the concerns voiced by the panel in 1962 — or perhaps more in response to the concerns — came many of the initial efforts that were made toward what has become known as career education.

For example, during the early to mid-1960s, the Richmond Plan, in which attempts were made to blend technical and trade education with general education, was developed by the Richmond (California) school system. In New Jersey, during the first half of the 1960s, the Technology for Children [T4C] Program, in which elementary school children were given a variety of experiences dealing with the world of work, was developed and implemented. The Western States Small Schools Project in the mid-1960s developed and used the concept of the Career Selection Program in order to help students in the smaller communities and high schools to develop an awareness of the world of work. The San Diego County schools during the same era developed and produced the View Program, which was designed to give the learner access to occupational information as it related to hundreds of occupations. There were also the efforts of the Pittsburgh schools, in which students were given an acquaintance with the world of work as well as experience in a real or simulated job situation.

The above are but a few of the programs that emerged during the 1960s in response to concerns such as those voiced by the Panel of Consultants on Vocational Education. Each of the programs was concerned with some aspect of what is now perceived as career education, and each in its own way was an immediate predecessor of the current concept. However, none of the efforts of the early and mid-1960s really attempted to "grasp the big picture" or to deal with the totality of the problem of helping every individual prepare for a satisfying and gratifying life career pattern. Instead, each seemed to address itself to a specific part or aspect of the "big picture." It was not until the late 1960s and early '70s that educational leaders began to grapple with the totality — or the perceived totality — of the problem.

In 1968, for example, the Advisory Council on Vocational Education (1968, p. xxiv), under the leadership of Martin W.

Essex, indicated that in addition to a basic commitment to provide vocational education, there were three other major areas of concern that should be considered as part of the totality of education:

> First, starting early in the student's formal education, he must learn more about work, its dignity, and his relationship to the occupational world. Actual work experiences need to be included as an integral part of the student's educational program....Second, the subject matter of the school and vocational requirements need to be realigned so that education becomes more meaningful in terms of its occupational potential. This involves a high degree of flexibility and a definite movement toward individualization of instruction....Third, the hardcore content of vocational education — the part that makes a person employable — must be adjusted to accommodate a wider range of occupational opportunity and a larger number of students.

Clearly, the elements of career education can be seen in the three areas of concern noted by the council.

Still further indications of the components of career education are to be seen in another closely related statement of the Advisory Council on Vocational Education (1968, p. xxiv):

> The renaissance in education must develop new relationships between the school and community at large to the end that education, with its vocational component, reaches into every facet of the community to provide for youth and adults now not being served.

It has already been suggested that it would be difficult if not impossible to trace *all* of the antecedents of career education. Those that have been briefly described here constitute but a few. It was, however, from antecedents such as these that the concept of career education as we know it today has developed.

The Concept, the Process, and the Product

The concept of career education, as it has been discussed in these pages, is from all indications a viable one — one that is both alive and healthy. This observation is given credence by numerous happenings in career education that have occurred since 1971. Nearly every state or territorial education agency, for example, now has a professional staff member who is responsible for career education efforts in the state or territory. In 1968, only one state had such a position. Some state legislatures in recent years have appropriated state monies to be used for the support of career education. And whereas a decade ago it was difficult to find professional publications that dealt with career education, today one can find many such publications.

Yet another evidence of support and acceptance of the concept of career education may be found in the numerous and extremely well-done plans, brochures, and other descriptive materials that have been developed by state education agencies for use in their own states. (Some of these are mentioned in the section of this and other chapters called "Selected References.")

Still further evidence of acceptance and support of the concept of career education may be found in the March 1974 issue of *Focus*, which is published by the National Association of State Boards of Education. It recently conducted a survey of educational priorities among state education agencies. Using a weighted formula to treat the state responses, the investigators found career education to be the highest priority. It should be noted that in one context, the survey indicated a need for or a concern about career education. Either expression, however, would tend to support the basic concept of career education.

Attacking the Issues

While there is fairly solid evidence that the *concept* is alive and well, there are indications that the *process* of career education is not so firmly fixed within the educational structure. This problem — to transform the concept into a process of career education — was addressed by chief state shool officers, USOE representatives, and others at a meeting in Pinehurst, North Carolina, April 1 to 3, 1974. At that meeting, Dr. Marland discussed with the participants some of the causal factors that tend to inhibit the implementation of career education on a broad scale and suggested that educational leaders from every level and aspect of education mount a concerted, cooperative effort to minimize the problems. Among the issues noted by Marland were those discussed in the following paragraphs.

Initiative: A major issue in almost any effort aimed at reform of one sort or another has to do with the matter of who should take the initiative. In the matter of career education, should the initiative be taken by the states, the federal government, or both? It would seem obvious that a harmoniously coordinated effort involving both would be the most productive.

Definition: The matter of definition — of occupational education, of vocational education, and of career education — continues to be an issue that contributes to the problem. This should not be a factor. Most educators have workable definitions for career education. While the definitions might differ in detail, it is in diversity that we might find workable solutions to the problems.

Passing fad: A major concern, notion, or idea shared by many is that career education is just another one of the educational changes that are proposed, accepted by some, and forgotten. Many people think that career education is not only here to stay but that it is also headed in the right direction. Nevertheless, the "passing fad" idea does contribute to the overall problem of implementation.

Articulation: There is a real need to develop strategies and procedures that will permit and encourage better articulation in all aspects and segments of the educational program. How can this best be accomplished? What are the preferable strategies and procedures? These are issues that must be resolved.

Territoriality: In education, each special interest group (vocational, general, or science education; industrial arts; and so on) has created its own empire and has been deeply committed to defending it. This is a thorny issue and significantly contributes to the problems relating to implementation of the process. In addition to territories that exist within the educational profession, there are other entities — such as the Departments of Agriculture, Transportation, Labor, Defense, the

Interior — which operate massive educational programs, and empires (or territories) exist there as well. Ways will have to be found to deemphasize the notion of "my territory" and of emphasizing cooperative approaches to common goals.

Funding: The issue of funding may perhaps be an aspect of territoriality. It is, however, a major concern or issue and is manifested in the concept of "This is our money, and...." If career education is to be the key to educational reform, substantial sums of money will be needed and ways must be found to convince all agencies that this is a crucial need. As an illustration of the magnitude of the amount of funding that could be used, we present the following breakdown:

(1) From an appropriation of $1 billion, each state could receive $20 million.

(2) From $1.5 billion, each school district could receive $100,000.

(3) A $5 billion appropriation would provide $100 for each student.

Contrast these figures with the *$15 billion* that is being used for welfare programs every year!

Anti-intellectualism: While to some, anti-intellectualism is "overdone," it nonetheless is a fact of our modern-day way of life. Too often, vocational education is perceived as a program for the less gifted or less able students. To some degree, territoriality may cause this attitude to surface. One might suggest, however, that much of it results from ignorance. Considerable educative effort is needed if this kind of ignorance is to be minimized or eliminated.

Minority concerns: There is a concern among many that career education may become just another way of tracking underachieving, culturally disadvantaged youngsters. Irrespective of the fact that career education, when functioning as it should, would actually serve to remove or lessen tracking, the concern is still a very real one and must be recognized. Efforts must be made to alleviate or minimize the concern.

Wait for research: There are those who would advocate that we wait until there is hard data from research to support the concept of career education; and this does present some problems. Sound bases for our actions are needed, and the use of research-based information to use in building the bases should be encouraged. However, it is possible to become bogged down, and a balance must be found.

Training or retraining of the teacher or counselor: In any area of educational reform, there is a need to orient — perhaps reorient — those affected by the change or reform. In the case of career education, two such groups are the teachers and the counselors. At the present time, not too many within these professions have had an opportunity to become actively involved in and trained for working in career education. This lack of involvement must be overcome if career education is to achieve its total potential.

Balancing educational programs with manpower needs: In the areas of occupational, vocational, and career education, there is a possibility of creating unrealistic expectations which, when unmet, can result in extreme frustrations. For example, it may be that some educational programs dealing with work opportunities are not appropriate in terms of manpower needs. The educational program — occupational, vocational, or career — must work closely with related agencies in order to ensure that imbalances between education and manpower needs are held to a minimum.

Summary

Obviously, there are other issues that might well be added to those suggested by career education advocates. Our purpose, however, was not that we identify *every* issue, for these will differ somewhat from state to state, city to city, and agency to agency. Instead, our purpose is to call attention to some problems and to suggest that all of them must be faced before the process of career education can be infused into existing educational programs.

Transforming the concept of career education into an operational process is one of the greatest challenges that education in America faces. As with other challenges that have been met, the task is not insurmountable. If the *process* can be implemented, the *product* will be found in the millions of people — young adults, mature adults, and elderly adults — who have had the benefit of someone helping them become the kind of person each *can* become.

Results of the Responses to the Questionnaire

Interestingly, the vitality, vigor, and acceleration of career education at the state and territorial levels would appear to be considerably healthier than has been suggested at the federal level. This, at least, is the impression one receives from examining the results of the recent questionnaire relating to the status of career education in several state and territorial educational jurisdictions.

The data from the questionnaires are reported in the following paragraphs. It should be emphasized at the outset, however, that the data given reflect only the returns (as of this writing) of 41 states and territories. This of course is nearly 75 percent, but it is not a complete sampling.

Priority Status of Career Education

Of the 41 states and territories, twelve have indicated — on a 1 to 5 descending scale — a high (1) priority for career education; fifteen have indicated a slightly less high (2) degree of priority. Six states showed a midpoint degree (3), while six others indicated a priority slightly less than midpoint (4), and one showed a low degree of priority (5). One state did not indicate a degree of priority for career education.

From the above, it is apparent that more than two-thirds (27) of the responding states and territories have given a priority for career education that is higher than midpoint. It is also apparent that these 27 states and territories are nearly half (48 percent) of the total (50 states and six territories) of the United States and its possessions. Thus the degree of priority and, by inference, the commitment to career education by state education agencies would appear to be significant.

Action Taken by State Education Agencies to Support Career Education

Because this aspect of the questionnaire deals with two variables — growth and total number — the results are shown below in tabular form. On the horizontal axis are the years in which the events or actions took place; the actions themselves are on the vertical axis. On the right vertical axis are the total number of actions in each category. As can be observed, there has been a fairly marked growth pattern — one that started slowly but which, since 1972, has accelerated sharply.

Action Taken	Year						
	'68	'69	'70	'71	'72	'73	Total
State board resolution		2		2	5	6	15
Position statement		1	2	1	13	10	27
State plan		2	3	1	4	18	28
Coordinator	1	2		3	12	15	33
Budget			1	4	4	9	18

Legislation Relating to Career Education

Of the 41 states and territories that responded to the questionnaire, fifteen either have legislation relating to career education or have initiated plans for such legislation. Seven of the responding states — Arizona, Arkansas, Connecticut, Florida, Louisiana, Ohio, and Washington — have indicated that actual legislation exists, while eight others said that some form of planning for career education legislation has taken place.

The remainder of the responding states said that no legislation existed. In several instances it was noted that such legislation was not needed to support career education, and in some instances it was suggested that legislation might actually be undesirable.

The answers to this section of the questionnaire would seem to reinforce the concept that every state is unique and that every state has different needs that require different measures.

Activities of the Council of Chief State School Officers

In addition to having acquired basic data on activities extant in the responding states and territories, those who processed the returned questionnaires were able to compile a list of activities that the respondents felt the Council could do to assist them in their career education efforts. In preferential order, they are as follows:

(1) Develop financial guidelines for career education

(2) Organize and conduct in-service programs for selected state education agency personnel

(3) Compile and disseminate information about state education agencies' efforts in:

(a) Curriculum modification

(b) Evaluation procedures

(c) Development of state career education plans

(4) Develop model legislation for career education

(5) Identify human and material resources

(6) Prepare, publish, and disseminate a position statement on career education

Activities of the U.S. Office of Education

In an attempt to gain further "directional" information, the questionnaire included a section in which the states and territories could indicate the kinds of activities that might be provided under the aegis of USOE to promote, encourage, support, and facilitate career education programs in the states and territories. These activities, in order of preference, are:

(1) In-service programs

(2) Curriculum development

(3) Funding of staff

(4) Dissemination efforts

(5) Special projects

(6) Funding of research and development

(7) Categorical funding for career education

Individual State Efforts

The questionnaire also asked states and territories to list activities which they had sponsored that encouraged or facilitated career education. From the information provided by the 41 respondents, it would appear that there has been a considerable degree of activity on the part of the state and territorial education agencies.

One state (Maryland) was actively involved in a series of some seventeen conferences on career education that were held across the nation since 1972. Governors' conferences, state conferences, and regional conferences have been held in several states. Workshops have been conducted in others. Funding for special or exemplary projects has been obtained in some states. Task forces or steering committees for career education have been established. At least one education agency (in Guam) has created an office of "assistant superintendent for career education." Other states have prepared and disseminated information in a variety of ways, including the preparation of slide-tape presentations, the issuance of newsletters, and the publication of explanatory booklets and a host of informative materials.

In short, considerable activity relating to career education has been initiated in several states. No attempt was made, however, to determine either degree or impact of the activities. Nor was any attempt made to determine the degree of implementation of career education programs in any of the local school systems.

Conclusions

The questionnaire represented an attempt to determine the present status of career education — to try to find out what is going on in the field. It obviously was not an in-depth study, and caution should be exercised in drawing any inferences or conclusions. The results, however, do indicate that across the nation career education is growing. But as with any growing organism, it will continue to need the kinds of support necessary to sustain its health and growth.

Selected References

Advisory Council on Vocational Education. *Vocational Education: The Bridge between Man and his Work.* Washington, D.C.: U.S. Department of Health, Education, and Welfare. 1968.

Arizona Department of Education. *Career Education: Leadership in Learning.* Phoenix: Arizona Department of Education. 1973.

Davenport, Lawrence; and Petty, Reginald. *Minorities and Career Education.* Columbus, Ohio: The House of Haynesworth. 1973.

Goldhammer, Keith; and Taylor, Robert E. *Career Education: Perspective and Promise.* Columbus, Ohio: Charles E. Merrill Books, Inc. 1972.

Herr, Edwin L. *Review and Synthesis of Foundations for Career Education.* Columbus, Ohio: ERIC Clearinghouse on Vocational and Technical Education. 1972.

Hoyt, Kenneth B.; *et al. Career Education and the Elementary School Teacher.* Salt Lake City: Olympus Publishing Company. 1973.

_____; *et al. Career Education: What It Is and How to Do It.* Second edition. Salt Lake City: Olympus Publishing Company. 1974.

Kunzman, Leonard E. *Career Education in Oregon.* Salem: Oregon State Board of Education. 1970.

Marland, Sidney P., Jr. "Career Education: A Report." Address to the National Association of Secondary School Principals, Washington, D.C., November 30, 1972.

_____. "Education for More than One Career." *World* (July 18, 1972).

_____. "Marland on Career Education." Washington, D.C.: U.S. Department of Health, Education, and Welfare. 1971. Reprinted from *American Education* (November 1971).

Maryland State Department of Education. "Career Education: Five-Year Action Plan." Baltimore: Maryland State Department of Education. 1972. Mimeographed.

McClure, Larry; and Buan, Carolyn. Editors. *Essays on Career Education*. Portland, Oregon: Northwest Regional Educational Laboratory. 1973.

Michot, Louis J. *State Plan for Career Education*. Baton Rouge: Louisiana State Department of Education. 1973.

National Association of State Boards of Education. *Focus*. Denver, Colorado: National Association of State Boards of Education. March 1974.

Nevada State Department of Education. *Career Development in Nevada*. Carson City: Nevada State Department of Education. 1973.

New Mexico State Department of Education. *Career Education in New Mexico*. Santa Fe: New Mexico State Department of Education. 1973.

Ohio Department of Education. *Career Motivation: Curriculum Guide for Grades K-6*. Columbus: Ohio Department of Education. 1972.

Ottina, John R. "Career Education Is Alive and Well." *Journal of Teacher Education* (Summer 1973).

Panel of Consultants on Vocational Education. *Education for a Changing World of Work*. Report of the Panel of Consultants on Vocational Education. Washington, D.C.: U.S. Office of Education. 1963.

Smith, Russell. *Career Education in Tennessee*. Nashville: Tennessee State Board of Vocational Education. 1973.

Turnbull, William W. Editor. *Proceedings of the Conferences on Career Education*. Princeton, New Jersey: Educational Testing Service. 1972.

Tyler, Gus. "Career Education and Society's Imperatives." In *Essays on Career Education*. Edited by Larry McClure and Carolyn Buan. Portland, Oregon: Northwest Regional Educational Laboratory. 1973.

2

Purposes and Goals of Career Education

David L. Jesser
Nancy M. Pinson*

When a society's conscience becomes aroused as a result
of the failure of one of its time-honored institutions to meet
or alleviate the concerns of that society for human wants and
needs, it becomes imperative for the institution to reexamine
its role and to reclarify its function. Such reexamination and
reclarification should of course be accomplished in a positive
manner and should result in the development of procedures
that enable the institution to marshal the resources — both
material and human — that are needed if the institution is to
respond more effectively to the concerns and needs of society.

The general statement above applies to all of the institutions which function within and are supportive of a society.
In the context of this discussion, however, it is intended to
apply more directly to the societal institution commonly re-
ferred to as the education system.

There are those who, in the modern-day era, would assert
that the schools — and the education system in general — have
failed to meet the concerns and needs of the society they have
been designed to serve. Parenthetically, it should be observed
that because of their public nature and exposure, schools are

---

*Specialist in Pre-Vocational Education and Career Development,
Maryland State Department of Education.

especially vulnerable to criticisms that are in effect manifesta-
tions of a societal conscience. However, regardless of vulner-
ability and susceptibility, when criticisms are voiced, the
schools must listen. And when such criticisms appear to be
justified, it is imperative that the schools reexamine their role
and reclarify their function.

But to make an assertion such as that above, without add-
ing several necessary qualifications, presents both the society
and the institution with an overly simplistic answer to a highly
complex problem. And unless the qualifications are considered,
the answer is likely to be shallow and unsatisfying. Answers
or probable solutions to problems in education have been fairly
numerous in nature, as has been noted in chapter 1. However,
as also noted, many of the "answers" have not resulted in substantive changes. They have, for the most part, been overly
simplistic answers to highly complex problems. They have not
in many instances recognized either the difficulties of assessing
broad profitability or the manner in which the school's output
related to the values held by the society. But fortunately, in
recent years there have been some reasoned and reasonable
approaches to ways in which schools might better face and
answer the criticisms being directed at them.

Some educators, who have moved beyond the easy criticism
of certain target anachronisms of their formal institutions,
have suggested that the schools look again at important learnings and important uses of those learnings. Lamm (1972), for
example, has viewed learning as laws and models of behavior
which, if valid, must be useful to the individual in social, accul-
turational, and personal economic contexts. Illich's basic faith
in "good" schooling (1970) is felt rather than spoken in his
belief that (educational) technology could be a servant of
independence and learning rather than the controller of bu-
reaucracy (and teaching), which it too often is.

McNally and Passon (1960) predicted that the resolution of
five issues would establish the "present" and future course of
education. Yet as we look at these questions today, it appears
that:

   (1) Schools have been more vocal about *social adjustment—*
       but continue to limit their self-assessment to reports
       of the intellectual status or "gain" of their students.

(2) Schools support the premise of interdisciplinary teaching and learning – but examples are hard to find in other than the elementary and middle school settings.

(3) Schools have made the socially acceptable choice between curriculum designed to adapt to a rapidly changing world and basic relatively unchanging subject matter – but are in conflict as to what those changes are to be.

(4) Schools have demonstrated both ability and conviction in the variety and number of procedures, resources, and tools they employ in response to local needs and local conditions

(5) Yet schools are still unresolved as to who is—and who shall make—the curriculum.

Schools always have expressed development of social skills, self-understanding, development of vocational competencies, self-actualization, and intellectual attainment as learning goals. But why is it that only in this last area any systematic attempt has been made to assess educational profitability? Perhaps it is because both schools and society have gradually assigned (and thereby confused the broader goals of) education to only the former agency, the schools, when these larger goals were once seen as shared by all of those institutions serving, if not also rewarding, human interests and needs. It should surprise no one that the school's concern about efficiency – in terms of the number and quality of educational services it could provide – has superseded the assessment of human profitability in self and social and vocational domains.

The critical dialogue between those who educate and prepare and those who well use and honor the schooled individual is only now beginning in earnest. Schools are facing the preeminent possibility that increments of positive gains in both teaching and learning will no longer suffice to satisfy a larger society which is demanding placement, higher gross national product, reduction of worker alienation, and a virtually utopian dream of low to no unemployment.

But ingress to the design and evaluation of educational services by extraschool agencies, institutions, and individuals is certain to cause conflict. Is integration possible? In Follet's words (Metcalf and Urwick, 1940), such a process will require a high order of intelligence, inventiveness, open-mindedness, perception, patience, and *time*. It is therefore imperative not only to limit the school's contribution to career education's goals as that which education and educators can realistically do — within the system — but also to actively seek and welcome the reinvolvement of other social institutions and the workplace itself in those educational functions which they are better equipped to provide. Such a coalition would not only release the creativity of its new members, but would elicit from them continual access to the only true settings in which to validate every goal of education.

It is reasonable to state, then, that when all of career education's goals are met, education's goals should be met in part— for if schools succeed in establishing themselves as particular, rather than exclusive, agents in the lifelong educational process, the reciprocal influence by many could perhaps achieve what too few have tried to do.

Purposes of Career Education

Whether career education was born of a need (1) to restructure American education because of public disaffection with it (revolution for the sake of revolution), or (2) to improve the quality of transition from education to employment (placement equating with societal and client forgiveness), or (3) to restore work as a viable and vital personal value (work as a means for self- and social reward, which contributes to both personal and economic independence), or none of these, the answers to these questions should be of less concern to us than the determinations we make about the role that educators must play in its effectiveness, its management, and its outcomes. While some of the previously cited definitions have described process, others have defined populations served (and those who serve them), and still others have stated outcomes in terms of desired human or programmatic goals. If none has succeeded in agreeing to who does what to (or for) whom with what observable results, all agree that career education is an effort (as opposed to an attitude), is a systematic effort in terms of an uninterrupted sequence of services, and is a systematic effort for all. And finally, this systematic effort for all shall ultimately be accountable through indices of meaning-fulness, growth, mobility, and fulfillment with and in the *work* one does throughout one's life.

Two recent statements, one by Goldhammer and Taylor and the other by Adelson, seem specifically appropriate to a discussion and consideration of the purposes and goals of career education. Goldhammer and Taylor (1972) have suggested that if the purposes of education are to have real meaning, they must be stated in terms of the individual learner and what he or she does as a result of participation in the educational process.

From the point of view that has been expressed, Gold-hammer and Taylor suggest that "the primary purpose of edu-cation is to assist the student to become a fully capacited, self-motivated, self-fulfilled, contributing member of society." As should be noted, this statement of purpose encompasses four essential concepts. Each concept should become one of the basic criteria for determining (1) *what* should happen to the learner, and (2) how the learner might demonstrate results of the "happening."

If an individual learner is to be fully capacitated, according to Goldhammer and Taylor, the school must make concerted effort to assist that individual—every individual—to acquire the skills and competencies needed to perform satisfactorily all of the roles the individual will likely assume during a life-time. This means that every individual must be equipped to adequately function in a variety of roles, and especially those that enable a person to:

(1) Make a contribution to the economic life of society, either as a producer of goods or a renderer of services

(2) Perform as a member of a family group

(3) Participate in the life of the community

(4) Participate in the avocational life of society

(5) Achieve competency in those activities of the com-munity that regulate the behaviors of its members and give meaning to the activities in which the citizens of the community engage

When an individual, as a result of participation in the educa-tional process, is equipped to adequately assume the roles or careers indicated above, the individual could be described as being "fully capacitated."

In addition to helping the individual be able to perform various roles in a satisfactory manner, however, the school (or education system) must also assist the individual in developing and maintaining the inner strength and drive needed to perform the various career roles in as effective a manner as possible. When an individual has the ability to maintain that strength and drive, the capability for self-motivation is likely to have been developed.

The third attribute that an individual should acquire as a result of participation in the educational process is self-fulfillment. When one has gained the ability to secure satisfactions and personal meaning from one's work and leisure activity, a degree of self-fulfillment will exist. Finally, "contributing" means that what an individual consciously does in life is a constructive force for the maintenance and improvement of the social body of which the individual is a part.

The second statement (Adelson, 1968) is equally valid and also relates to the purposes of education. Adelson suggests that an education should equip an individual to want well, inquire effectively, evaluate carefully, understand extensively, and enjoy deeply. Where Goldhammer and Taylor used four basic concepts on which to build their statement, Adelson chose to use five. Yet within a broad construct, both are valid statements of purpose for the present-day education system. Both have gone far beyond the concept that education consists of the collection, assimilation, and dissemination of a variety of seemingly unrelated and unconnected bits of information. To the contrary, both statements represent a point of view which pleads for an education system that is simultaneously more relevant and responsive to the needs of the individual.

According to Adelson (as with Goldhammer and Taylor), a person must be able (or equipped) to do something as a result of participating in the educational process. He defined that "something" in the following manner (p. 238):

> A person must learn to extract from the world all that is most relevant to his life, to avail himself of the opportunities life offers, to avoid its dangers, and to deal with its situations as they arise. He must be

able to organize what he learns, to enjoy the knowledge whenever possible, to use it in formulating and solving problems, and to employ it in discerning and seizing opportunities. He must be able to implement appropriate action whatever his situation. To some extent, all these functions must be performed in anticipation of those outcomes which can be influenced by his own behavior.

The purposes that Goldhammer, Taylor, and Adelson have ascribed to the educational process and education system may not appear to differ in any marked way from other statements of goals and purposes that have been developed during the first two-thirds of the twentieth century. Indeed, they are eminently acceptable. However, it must be noted that so also have been the formulations of the 1918 Commission of Reorganization of Secondary Education, the 1938 Educational Policies Commission, and the 1944 Conference on the Imperative Needs of Youth, to mention but a few. Few substantive changes in education have resulted from these goal statements. Perhaps the purposes have not been understood.

Goals of Career Education

Whether education or career education is the topic, the purposes that are ascribed or assigned require that something must happen before the purposes can be achieved. Certain things, happenings, or activities are implied by the purposes. Educational leaders, regardless of their level of operation, must recognize that every statement of purpose — if it is thoughtfully formulated — will have implications that lead to specific actions or to courses of action, and they must be prepared to accept such implications.

Bebell, in an insightful and perceptive examination of the goals and purposes of education (1968), has suggested that the changing purposes of education will require growth in (1) curriculum, (2) instruction, (3) instructional improvement practices, (4) supporting services, (5) evaluation, (6) teacher education, and (7) continuing education. The implications suggested by Bebell have rather obvious significance in any discussion of the purposes and goals of career education because they

also begin to respond to the *who* does *what* portion of any goal
statement – a portion which is too often omitted at the cost
of the recipient (who) and his or her acquired behavior (the
observable result). They will be examined here in conjunction
with their potential and dynamic affiliation with the purposes
and goals of career education.

Curriculum

The curriculum aspect of career education has two components: the who and the what.

Who: The curriculum – seen broadly as not only the classroom teacher and the materials and procedures that he or she
employs, but as an identified fabric of human beings drawn
from both the institution of home and family and the business,
labor, and industry community – will indicate an enrichment
of educational "text" which can begin to more effectively relate
the acquisition of knowledge to its rewarded appearance in
the larger society.

What: The basic disciplines, whose command is necessary
for them to function adequately, if not distinctively, in a world
where higher "value" is being placed upon the habit of or the
capacity for acquiring new and yet-to-be-defined competencies
will need to convey:

(1) The utility of basic arithmetic skills in situations where
one must conserve, spend, barter, or build, as well as
where one must solve an immediate computational task
stated as a classroom exercise

(2) The utility of basic communications skills in situations
where one must persuade, defend, inspire, encourage,
or translate, as well as where one must communicate
a given idea

(3) The utility of basic scientific principles in situations
where one must work with or modify existing environmental elements, as well as where one must replicate
a known scientific formula

(4) The utility of basic social science principles in situations
where one must deal with current social attitudes,

habits, and needs, as well as where one must articulate a synthesis of the world's cultures

(5) The utility of basic physiological principles in situations where one must match psychomotor skills with the ongoing maintenance, improvement, and task appropriateness of those skills, as well as where one must achieve mastery over a given physical challenge

Instruction

Although instruction, as we see it, encompasses only one element — the who — that one is fourfold: the student, the teacher, the home and family, and the business, labor, and industry community.

Who: Implicit in the broader definition of curriculum is the instructional involvement of those who are now seen as integral to its design:

(1) *The student:* Student participation would not be limited, for example, to a voiced approval (by the student) of a "good" curriculum but would extend even the inquiry and discovery methods to include peer instruction and guidance, as well as having access to the design and selection of materials and experiences.

(2) *The teacher:* The teacher is, and must remain, the single most important coordinator of instructional services, resources, and materials. The changing characteristics of these procedures and "tools," as defined by career education's emphasis upon humanizing the curriculum by bringing more kinds of people into the educational process, will require that teachers reexamine their own teaching styles. Individualization of instruction would not only involve greater use of teaching aids and supporting services (and a companion reduction in the lecture techniques) but would presuppose the teacher's own acquisition of skills in interdisciplinary and interagency team processes, applied knowledge in the realms of human development and guidance, and competencies in those kinds of instructional evaluations which stress human processes and conditions, as

well as terminal demonstrations of skill or content assimilation.

(3) *The home and family:* The most pervasive and most durable influence upon the aspirations, values, and attitudes of its members is the home and family. This element can be instrumental in the personal, physical, and verbalized delivery to all students of a cultural and societal microcosm that reflects what *is* — thus the students learn to know and respect precedents, even as they formulate variations upon them.

(4) *The business, labor, and industry community:* The involvement of this aspect of the student's life will no longer be seen as that random on-the-job training which places the employer and the employee in essentially reactive (and defensive) positions. Readiness of the workplace for that individual who will have acquired purposefulness and self-esteem as well as generalized skills of "employability" can occur only if the employing community is involved early enough and constantly enough in the educational process to recognize and provide for needed changes in the nature of work itself.

Summary

We have now looked at curriculum and instruction in terms of that particular coalition of school, home, and family and the business, labor, and industry community — all of which, given time and educational portfolio, could accomplish the goals of career education in full, and those of education in part. These change agents are the *real*, as opposed to the elusive *who* in the assignment of shared responsibilities in the provision of career education's programs, services, processes, and resources.

Yet no discussion of career education's goals should fail to take into account two component processes which fall within the purview (if not the sole dominion) of two uniquely qualified domains in education. While guidance has traditionally been assigned a "supporting service" role in education, its centrality to the process of career education requires a reassessment of its unexploited potential. In any statement of the *what* of an instructional program or procedure (whether it be career education or environmental education), it is essential that a mechanism or system recognizing the variability or human response, error, or growth be inserted to reinforce and protect the learner as he or she reacts to, adapts, synthesizes, and internalizes portions of any externally imposed experience.

This system is correctly identified with the guidance or counselor function, and in the case of career education is further refined as that which is concerned with the maximum career development of the individual. As a "process," this term is best defined as that which occurs within the individual over a lifetime as he or she reflects upon, reacts to, rejects, or acts upon cumulative experiences he, she, or others have designed which are presently or ultimately related to self and work values, aspirations, behaviors, and skills.

Because optimum career development is viewed as a goal of career education, the career guidance component which facilitates it is seen as a major responsibility of the entire constellation of student services. Not only will these uniquely trained individuals generate activities which permit students to acquire skills in decision making, work value clarification, and self-assessment, they will extend these and other skills to teachers, parents, and the community at large.

Vocational Skills

A second domain of crucial importance to both the *who* (does) and the *what* (is) of career education is the vocational skills development process. It is important to make the distinction here between this process and that of vocational education, one of its integral parts. The process itself includes each increment of affective and psychomotor skill which can be directly associated with the precursors of vocational competency and maturity. In this respect, the hand never becomes dissociated from the mind and body, and the individual's translation of ideas to concrete and visible products is as correctly used by the future chemist when he or she first transfers the contents of one test tube to another as when the future chef is allowed the run of a kitchen.

All learning, and all who provide it, will therefore be involved in this process, while at a certain level of readiness for particular occupationally related skills, teachers — who are equipped to provide experience in and knowledge, competencies, and attitudes inherent to those occupational fields — will find their students basing career and occupational choices upon an acquired "history" of self-knowledge, exploratory experiences, and goal-setting behaviors.

Components of Career Education

Many excellent pictorial or graphic models of career education's goals have been developed over recent months. To choose among these is difficult because of the detail and scope of some and the overly general nature of others. However, there seems to be agreement between the progenitors of outcome statements that good career education will result in those individuals who are not only motivated and prepared to work but have the power and the knowledge to create (if they cannot find) those work settings perceived as personally rewarding to their changing and developing talents, interests, and abilities.

The matrix in Figure 2.1, developed by Pinson, attempts to illustrate the five components of career education as elements contributing to particular and collective contributions to career education's goal for the individual. While it does not attempt to describe program elements or characteristics (which will be discussed in a later chapter of this book) and does not develop an extensive list of existing behavior at given points of departure from one educational or maturational level to another, it may be useful to the reader in placing the fabric of career education in perspective.

In bringing this discussion to a close, we remind the reader of the oft-voiced concern of school-level personnel who must ultimately be responsible for the coordination of those resources, services, and personnel identified as integral to the delivery of career education. When broad goals are stated and existing behaviors described, they should not be seen as exclusive to certain age levels or as transition points in education. Entering high school students, for example, are as entitled to modifications of those experiences which would have been pre-

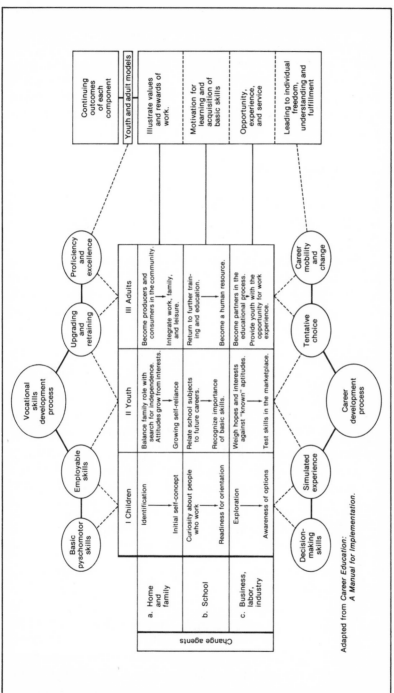

Figure 2.1. The Five Components of Career Education

Adapted from *Career Education: A Manual for Implementation*.

sented to them when they were elementary-age children as retired adults would be in gaining acess to the exploration of a number of careers which were not in existence during their youth.

With these cautions in mind, let us sample interim goal statements — which imply a gradual increase in all individuals' power to predict, forecast, assess, and plan their present and future in terms of the work they do or will do.

The Awareness Stage

By the end of the elementary school years, or at the close of the initial stage of career education, students should be able to:

(1) Demonstrate appreciation of the reasons people select a career; appreciation toward work itself as a means of achieving many satisfactions and toward work in relation to themselves — as they see it now and as they "predict" its importance in their futures

(2) Demonstrate an understanding of the life-styles, values, major duties, and responsibilities involved in a broad range of career areas

(3) Express their interests in terms of their relatedness to adult hierarchies of work and leisure behaviors

(4) Demonstrate their ability to relate the acquisition of basic skills of communication and computation to the successful engagement of a multitude of future roles

(5) Begin to think well of themselves in terms of each one's unique potential as a future member of a service-oriented society

(6) Begin to develop a set of work values that holds personal meaning for them

The Investigation and Decision-Making Stage

At the end of their middle or junior high school experience, or at the close of an exploratory and sampling stage, students should be able to:

(1) Demonstrate a knowledge of their interests and talents, along with demonstrable basic decision-making skills

(2) Demonstrate an in-depth knowledge of several major career fields

(3) Demonstrate an awareness of many additional career fields they would like to investigate

(4) Explore and express their own values, interests, and educational achievements

(5) Have a firsthand experience with the economic system — as consumers and as observers of those who work to produce goods and perform services

(6) Select a tentative high school educational plan best suited to their individual needs and desires

(7) Integrate knowledge of self and of the world of work in order to identify a career or careers for which they have made tentative decisions

Goals of the Preparation Stage

In addition to the continuing outcomes of previous levels, students who have spent time exploring self in work should be able to:

(1) Seek and use the specific training opportunity they describe as appropriate to their goals

(2) Become gainfully employed at an entry level appropriate to their career objectives upon leaving high school

(3) Enter a community college, technical institute, preparatory school, apprenticeship program, senior college, or some other high school occupational or further educational training setting

(4) Recognize the changing nature of career commitment through an individual's lifetime — by knowing how to reevaluate initial career choices, to state alternative choices, and to seek the experience and training necessary for their implementation

These, then, are the purposes and goals of career education as we see them.

Selected References

Adelson, Marvin. "Educational Ends and Means." In *Inventing Education for the Future.* Edited by Werner Hirsche. San Francisco: Chandler Publishing Company. 1968.

Bebell, Clifford S. F. "The Educational Program." In *Emerging Designs for Education.* Edited by Edgar L. Morphet and David L. Jesser. New York: Citation Press. 1968.

Goldhammer, Keith; and Taylor, Robert. *Career Education: Perspective and Promise.* Columbus, Ohio: Charles E. Merrill Books, Inc. 1972.

Goulder, Alvin W. "Cosmopolitans and Locals: Toward an Analysis of Latent Social Roles." *Administrative Science Quarterly* (1957), vol. 2.

Hoyt, Kenneth B.; *et al. Career Education and the Elementary School Teacher.* Salt Lake City: Olympus Publishing Company. 1973.

Illich, Ivan. *Deschooling Society.* New York: Harper & Row, Publishers, Incorporated. 1970.

Lamm, Z. "The Status of Knowledge in the Radical Concept of Education." In *Curriculum and the Cultural Revolution.* Edited by David E. Purpel and Maurice Belanger. Berkeley, California: McCutchan Publishing Company. 1972.

Leibermann, M. "An Overview of Accountability." *Phi Delta Kappan* (1970), vol. 52, no. 4.

McNally, H. J.; and Passon, A. H. *Improving the Quality of Public School Programs.* New York: Teachers College Press. 1960.

Metcalf, Henry C.; and Urwick, Lyndall. Editors. "The Collected Papers of Mary Parker Follett." In *Dynamic Administration.* New York: Harper & Brothers. 1940.

Pinson, Nancy M. *Career Education: A Manual for Implementation.* Washington, D.C.: U.S. Office of Education. 1972.

3
The Development
and Use of
Curriculum Materials
for Career
Education

David L. Jesser
Linda Keilholtz*

Since the beginning of the initial developmental efforts in career education in the early 1960s, considerable attention has been devoted to ways in which educational institutions might better respond to the needs of the learner in terms of career development. The attention and effort have been bolstered by resources provided by private foundations, by efforts of federal and state government agencies, and by provisions of federal laws. For example, provisions of the vocational education amendments of 1968 have enabled state and local education agencies to design, plan for, and implement many exemplary career education programs.

Other appropriations relating to the same legislation have made it possible for other federal and state agencies to support career education efforts in several similar ways. In 1971, for example, USOE allocated resources for the development of "modules" that could be useful in implementing career education. Funds, under Parts C and D of the vocational education amendments, were also made available for the purpose of encouraging and supporting the development of exemplary career education programs in every state. And funds, especially under

---

*Supervisor of Career Development for Ohio State Department of Education.

Part I, were provided for the purpose of developing certain types of curricular materials.

The efforts under Part I of the vocational education amendments did not "just happen"; they emerged from a need which became all too apparent when efforts were made to bring career education into the total curriculum. In some instances, as with several of the fifteen occupational clusters (Hoyt *et al.*, 1974, pp. 31–32, 95), suitable curricular materials were found to be lacking. As a result, as thrusts to implement career education within the existing school structure have taken more definitive form, it has become essential for serious thought to be given to practicable ways in which this new dimension of education might best be implemented.

At the outset, it appeared that some fundamental changes in education would have to occur if implementation of career education were to be achieved. Several options — or possible changes — seemed apparent. These included:

(1) The existing school day could be lengthened in order to accommodate career education.

(2) Significant portions of the existing curriculum could be deleted and replaced by career education.

(3) A deliberate effort could be made to revise curricular materials in local school districts in order that they might retain essential existing materials, but at the same time career development could be incorporated.

As claims that the existing curriculum was irrelevant became more prominent, and as more and more people asserted that the curriculum did not meet the needs of students for either the present or the future, the nation's education agencies began to seriously consider the third option. They were able to perceive career education as the change agent which could both reorient and revitalize the heavily criticized existing curriculum.

Role of Curriculum in Career Education

In general, career education programs have tended to emphasize the use of various types of career-oriented classroom activities as one method of relating traditional subject matter to the world of work. Initial efforts often consisted of providing students with field trip experiences and of inviting community resource people into the classroom to discuss their own careers with the students. It became apparent, however, to career education advocates that the goals which had been envisioned for career education could not be reached without an articulated, integrated approach. It became apparent to its proponents that career education, if it were to be a truly moving force in American education, could not be simply another manifestation of the "add-on" syndrome that has so often afflicted education — a point emphasized by Hoyt and his colleagues (1974, p. 159):

> Career education does not ask the academic classroom teacher to simply add one or more units to an already overcrowded set of learning objectives. Rather, it asks the teacher to change and adapt current lesson plans to accommodate a career education emphasis.

But is it possible and feasible for curriculums to be modified so that they incorporate or integrate the concepts of career education?

The extent to which schools with identifiable career education programs were able to integrate career development concepts into existing curriculums was the subject of nationwide study conducted in 1972 by the Center for Occupational Education at North Carolina State University. In the course of the study, funded by a grant from USOE, 41 schools and their programs were reported and described in a publication (Morgan et al., 1972). In virtually every program description, there are to be found clear indications that strong emphasis had indeed been placed on the integration of career development concepts into the curriculum.

In a later document prepared by the North Carolina Center (Morgan et al., 1973), fifteen of the 41 programs which had been visited were analyzed in depth. In each analysis, a section was devoted to an examination of how the educational program had been used to support the career education concept. Again, the emphasis on the integration of career development concepts into the overall educational program was readily apparent.

In several other USOE–sponsored efforts, the importance of the role of the curriculum in implementing the concept of career education has been repeatedly stressed. Two statements prepared by the American Institutes for Research in the Behavioral Sciences (which have been engaged in the development of curricular materials for use in career education) serve to illustrate this emphasis (Dunn, 1973, p. 4):

> [1] During the early part of this century, the curriculum was defined largely in terms of its social utility, that is, in terms of its benefits to society as a whole. During the 1930s and 1940s curriculum attention centered largely on the consideration of principles of child growth and development. During the 1950s and 1960s curriculum development was concerned almost exclusively with content considerations. In recent years, however, one can begin to see a growing emphasis on *personal* utility.... [2] The increasing sophistication of education in accommodating individual differences, in personal interests, abilities, goals, and ambitions, coupled with the growing social concern for the maintenance of individuality in an increasingly dehumanized and technological society, appears to be resulting in a strong pressure for schools to become more concerned with serving the individual.

From the evidence available, it is apparent that the curriculum can be the single most effective delivery system available to schools as they implement programs of career education. However, it should be equally apparent that the curriculum should reflect the changes which concepts of career education demand through a totally articulated conceptual design. It must *not* be merely "another" curriculum.

Impact of Career Education on State and Local Curriculum Development

As a result of the needs indicated, the promise of career education has already had considerable impact on curriculum development efforts in almost every state in the nation. In many instances, funds have been made available by USOE for the purpose of helping states and local school systems conceptualize and develop career education curriculum designs to meet their own needs. In some instances, state funds have been made available for these purposes, and local education agencies have been encouraged to develop curriculum materials which would supplement, if not replace, existing textbooks and other curriculum materials which did not contain concepts of career education.

It has been observed that while there has been considerable progress in the area of curriculum development for career education at the national level, the rate of progress has varied somewhat from one effort to another. In terms of state effort in curriculum development, the same general observations would seem appropriate. Some state education agencies have perceived the area of curriculum development for career education to be a function of the agency and consequently have developed materials suitable for use in their individual programs. On the other hand, some state education agencies have not yet become involved.

Obviously, if there is no perceived need, these agencies should not become involved. Curriculum development can be tedious, time consuming, and costly. And these education agencies should certainly not become involved in curriculum development merely for the sake of "being involved." If, however, after carefully examining the existing curricular resources, the state education agency does perceive a real need for additional (or substitute or curricular) materials, it is possible for relevant and useful materials to be produced.

In New Mexico, where the primary focus of career education in 1973–74 was directed toward kindergarten through sixth grade, there was an obvious need for curriculum materials that would assist elementary school teachers in integrating career education concepts into the existing curriculum. No suitable materials of this nature were available. As a result, under the leadership of Dr. Jean Page, of the New Mexico Department of Education, a set of some five hundred career education "activity cards," for use by individual teachers, was developed and distributed to the elementary schools. These should provide the teachers with a valuable tool to use in career education. A sample card is shown in Figure 3.1.

When a career development program was planned in Ohio, it was apparent that teachers would need some assistance, in the form of curricular materials, if the concepts of career education were to be successfully integrated into the existing cur-

Grade Level 2 Hospitality Cluster   Language Arts   Creative Arts
 Activity . . . . "Park Design" You like to play in a park. Can you think of any jobs that people have at the park? Who keeps it looking nice? Design a park you would like. Suggested Materials Cardboard, popsicle sticks, clay, construction paper, metal, rocks

Figure 3.1. New Mexico's Sample Activity Card
for Career Education

riculum. As a result, three major curriculum guides, "Career Motivation" (K–6), "Career Orientation" (grades 7 and 8), and "Career Exploration" (grades 9 and 10), have been developed under the leadership of Dr. Byrl Shoemaker, Ohio State Director of Vocational Education. Figures 3.2 and 3.3 show the type of material developed for kindergarten through sixth grade. In the Ohio materials, the teacher is presented with information relating to topic, behavioral objectives, suggested activities, and sample lessons.

While the illustrations of the New Mexico and Ohio efforts are directed toward the K–6 segment of education, it should be noted that similar efforts have been made for the middle and secondary segments of education as well in several states. In Oregon, for example, curricular materials have been developed for use in the various occupational clusters that have been identified as being applicable in the Oregon effort. These occupational cluster guides contain information relating to students' tasks and objectives, to the principles of the specific learning activity, to required knowledge or skills, and to suggested activities. A representative example of the Oregon career education cluster guide is shown in Figure 3.4.

The Individual and His Environments

DEVELOPMENTAL OBJECTIVE

To develop an awareness of work in the society.

RELATED BEHAVIORAL OBJECTIVES

1. Given a situation in which the children trace a product through its entire production, they will be able to name the workers involved in this production and the tasks they performed.

2. Given a field trip to a company which produces some product, the child will be able to see products and relate what he has seen to one other person.

SUGGESTED ACTIVITIES

1. Ask the children to list the foods they ate for breakfast. Have them take the list home to find out where the product was boxed and packaged.

2. Role play a situation showing how a product is produced (e.g., how a loaf of bread is made), and use the children to portray all of the workers involved in its production.

3. Give the students an assignment made up of several steps in incorrect order. Have them organize the steps in proper order, set up a "production line" and carry the assignment through to completion. Have them describe difficulties encountered in the process.

ADDITIONAL ACTIVITIES

Source: Ohio State Department of Education, *Career Motivation: Curriculum Guide for Grades K-6*, 1972.

Figure 3.2. Developmental Project from Ohio's "Career Motivation" Curriculum Guide (K–6)

Our using curricular materials from three states only in no way implies that other states have not developed career education materials. These examples are merely to illustrate that interest in this area has been shown by some states; but pro-

---

SAMPLE LESSON

"Go Fly a Kite"

MATERIALS

See below

PROCEDURE

1. Discuss with the class types of work done on a production line basis. Follow this with a film showing a production line in operation (e.g., put out by Ford Motors, Proctor & Gamble, etc), or visit a plant in which a production line exists.

2. Discuss details of setting up an assembly line for kite making in the classroom.

3. Provide the following materials to be used in the production line in the classroom: kite sticks of two different lengths, tissue paper (colored, pre-cut), string, cloth scraps, glue, scissors.

4. Put these directions on the board in any order, and read them to the class:

   a. Sort materials and put them in the correct order of assembly.

   b. Tie the sticks together.

   c. Glue tissue paper to sticks.

   d. Tie flying string to crossbar.

   e. Cut cloth into strips.

   f. Tie cloth strips to tail string.

   g. Go Fly a Kite!

5. Have children put directions in correct order, designate jobs, and complete production line task.

6. Evaluate the results.

NOTES AND COMMENTS

Source: Ohio Department of Education, *Career Motivation: Curriculum Guide for Grades K-6*, 1972.

Figure 3.3. Sample Lesson from Ohio's "Career Motivation" Curriculum Guide (K-6)

Required Knowledge and Skills	The Student Can	Suggested Learning Activities
The occupational opportunities in horticulture	Identify common horticultural plants found in the community.	Propagate plants in a greenhouse.
The types of horticultural businesses and their product or services: (a) greenhouse production, (b) nursery production, (c) turf production, (d) landscaping, (e) fruit production, (f) vegetable production	Propagate plants, using seed and various propagating media.	Take cuttings; root and transplant.
	Propagate plants vegetatively by cutting, graftage, budding, and layering.	Conduct field trips to commercial greenhouses and nurseries.
	Transplant plants from seedling flats to growing-out containers.	Prune fruit trees in a home orchard.
Factors and methods of propagating plants by: (a) seeds, (b) division, (c) layering, (d) cuttings, (e) grafting, (f) budding	Prepare a soil mix for use in the greenhouse.	Trim and shape shrubs on the school grounds.
	Operate equipment used in a nursery, greenhouse, landscaping firm, or fruit or vegetable farm.	Landscape an area of the school grounds.
Essential equipment and its use in propagation of plants		
The purpose and effects of pruning trees, shrubs, and vines	Prepare and plant a lawn. (Land lab or around school grounds or home.)	
The common ornamental plants grown in the community	Outline a lawn maintenance program.	
Methods and equipment used in planting seeds and bulbs	Sketch a simple plot plan.	
Methods of culturing bedding and potted plants	Read a landscape plan and install prescribed plants.	

Source: Oregon Board of Education, *Occupational Cluster Guide: Agriculture* (1970).

Figure 3.4. Oregon's Occupational Cluster Guide

gress in this area of career education has been varied. The materials used herein are intended to reflect some of that progress.

Accountability and Evaluation

As state and local education agencies became increasingly involved in curriculum development, there emerged a real need for intensive in-service educational programs which would aid personnel in acquiring the skills necessary for effective curriculum development, including abilities to write sequential as well as measurable objectives. As a result, in-service programs which have considerable emphasis on the evaluation of career-oriented curricular materials have been developed and implemented in several states. With these efforts, the need for understanding and accepting accountability in curriculum development has become an integral part of curriculum design. This is illustrated by a statement of the North Carolina Career Education Task Force (1973, p. 31) in support of this crucial area of concern — evaluation and accountability:

Evaluation by school personnel is concerned with finding what is done in the school with students and how change may be brought about to help them realize their potentials as completely as possible. The evaluation process should be guided by the objectives for learners as outlined in a comprehensive curriculum plan. The evaluation of the sum total of the learner's progress can be directly related to the school's progress in planning and accreditation.... With a career education emphasis in the curriculum, a variety of techniques of evaluation must be used to determine its effectiveness. In essence this evaluation is ... of the entire curriculum. We have traditionally used formal tests ... as the main instrument of evaluation [but] we must include other forms ... including use of interviews, anecdotal records, experience diaries [and] checklists.... However, there must be a common format and uniformity of application. Teachers, in particular, need to know a great deal about evaluation and how to use evaluation techniques.... There is a need to go beyond the measuring of information learned and skills acquired. There is concern with the kinds of habits and attitudes children are forming. The question of concepts, thinking ability, interests, appreciations, and personal adjustment must be considered. Additionally, the extent to which the student is using and applying knowledge and skills must be evaluated.... Finally, we must remember that the *primary* purpose of evaluation is the improvement of teaching and learning.

Almost most of the state and locally developed curricular materials have not been used for a sufficient period of time or have not been controlled so that they provide for thorough validation procedures, many of the materials have been widely disseminated. In addition, USOE has published and distributed several career education bibliographies, and listings of career education curriculum materials have been compiled by organizations such as the Center for Vocational and Technical Education at the University of Ohio, the North Carolina Center, the American Institutes for Research in the Behavioral Sciences, and by various state education agencies. Such materials serve to illustrate the depth and breadth of career-oriented curricular materials that are being developed and produced.

National Efforts in Career Education Curriculum Development

In recent years, USOE has funded numerous curriculum development projects in efforts to make validated and transportable curriculum materials available to state and local education agencies. A significant example is the school-based career education model that was developed by the Center for Vocational and Technical Education (CVTE) of Ohio State University. Although it has since been transferred for monitoring to the recently organized National Institute of Education, the CVTE project developed, among other items, a matrix which provided a scope and sequence of goal statements appropriate for kindergarten through twelfth grade. The CVTE process began with the identification of eight elements of career education — self-awareness, education awareness, career awareness, economic awareness, decision making, beginning competency, employable skills, and attitudes and appreciation — which were used to define the concept of career education. The eight basic elements were further defined in 32 themes.

The document that was developed illustrates the elements, the themes, and the appropriate goal statements. The goal statements were later used in the development and revision of curriculum units. The CVTE efforts strove to modify existing curriculums in attempts to build an articulated curriculum system in kindergarten through twelfth grade. CVTE has more recently developed and published a rather extensive listing of career education curriculum materials (Ohio State University, 1973) in which units appropriate for use in each of the eight basic elements are described.

Staff development: The need for in-service training opportunities for educators who are beginning to use the newly developed curricular materials has already been noted. Toward this end, CVTE has also been engaged in the development of a series of in-service training products that are designed to support the implementation of a comprehensive career education program. CVTE in-service materials include five categories: (1) advisory committee materials, (2) in-service coordinators' materials, (3) general orientation to career education materials, (4) specific audience role orientation materials, and (5) special and ongoing staff development materials. These are described in terms of focus, intended users, and availability in a recent Center publication, *Staff Development Products* (1973).

American Institutes for Research in Behavioral Sciences: Another significant effort, supported with funds provided by USOE, is the attempt of the American Institutes for Research in the Behavioral Sciences to develop validated sample career education materials for kindergarten through ninth grade. The Institutes' efforts, illustrated in Figure 3.5, are intended to provide the user with an array of instructional objectives from which to choose in order to implement a career-oriented curriculum.

U.S. Office of Education's fifteen career clusters: In still another USOE attempt to aid in the development and implementation of career-oriented curriculum, efforts were made to refine the nearly 25,000 titles in the *Dictionary of Occupa-*

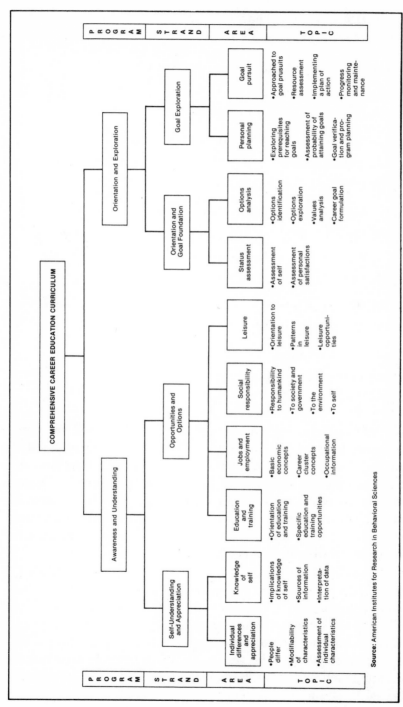

Figure 3.5. The AIR Career Education Curriculum Topic Chart

tional Titles (various years). As a result, fifteen occupational
or career clusters were identified:

(1) Agri-business and natural resources

(2) Business and office

(3) Communications and media

(4) Consumer and homemaking education

(5) Construction

(6) Environmental control

(7) Fine arts and humanities

(8) Health

(9) Hospitality and recreation

(10) Manufacturing

(11) Marine science

(12) Marketing and distribution

(13) Personal services

(14) Public services

(15) Transportation

Within the framework of this structure, which was far more
manageable and less cumbersome than the separate job titles
in the dictionary, a series of grants was made for development
of curriculum materials to be used in specific clusters. Grants
were made for curriculum development projects in the area of
occupations in public services, business and office, marketing
and distribution, manufacturing, construction, communications and media, and transportation clusters.

As might be expected in an effort as massive and diverse as
curriculum development for the various occupational clusters,
progress has varied. In several of the occupational clusters, as
well as in other federally funded curriculum projects, significant
progress has been made. Several of these — including those
having to do with public service occupations, elementary curriculum, technology, and minority students — are briefly described in the following section.

Public Service Occupations Curriculum Project

The Public Service Occupations Curriculum Project, one of several funded under Part I of the vocational education amendments of 1968, was initiated in the fall of 1971. Since that time, it has been engaged in the development of nationally applicable curriculum guidelines and materials for one of the fifteen career clusters. The effort, under the direction of Dr. Patrick J. Weagraff of the vocational section of the California State Department of Education, has resulted in the development and field testing of several curricular approaches that can be used in conjunction with this particular cluster.

Public Service Analysis

As the project became operational and as the project staff began to develop its detailed plans, it became evident that considerable variations were to be found in existing definitions of "public service." It was therefore decided that a fundamental step in the development of an appropriate secondary-level curriculum for the public service career field would be an acceptable definition of the term "public service." The project staff, with the help of a group with expertise in local, state, and federal governmental operations as well as secondary and post-secondary education, made a rather thorough analysis and ultimately adopted as its guide the following definition (Weagraff, 1973, p. 11):

> Public service occupations are those occupations pursued by persons performing the functions necessary to accomplish the mission of local, county, state, and federal government, excluding the military service and trades requiring an apprenticeship. These missions reflect the services desired or needed by individuals and groups ... and are performed through arrangements or organizations established by society, normally on a nonprofit basis and usually supported by tax revenues.

On the basis of the above description, the project staff and the advisory groups were able to identify eight major occupational groups and 39 major job families in the public service field. The major groups and families (shown in Figure 3.6), in the view of the project staff, adequately reflect the several discrete governmental functions that are performed at local, state, and federal levels.

Curriculum Guidelines

Using the eight major occupational groups and the 39 major job families as bases for consideration, the project staff organized and developed several sets of curriculum guidelines for use in secondary schools. The first set, *Orientation to Public Service Occupations* (1973), was designed to acquaint secondary school students with public service and to help the students answer questions such as:

(1) What is public service?

(2) What does it offer me?

(3) What are the requirements for jobs?

(4) How much can I earn?

In addition, the orientation guide contains a separate section for each major occupational group, making it a useful resource for teachers who are concerned with implementation of the concept of career education.

The project has developed a second set of guidelines in which students are provided with information about elementary job skills. This set, *Preparing for Public Service Occupation: Common Core* (1973), uses a "common core" and includes: oral communications, written communications, basic report writing, basic record keeping, good grooming, relationships with other people, interviewing skills, applying for public service jobs, and techniques of decision making. Each of these is applicable to any type of career development; hence the term "common core."

Both sets of guidelines make use of the unit approach, and each is intended to be highly adaptable to various types of learning situations. Because each unit is self-contained, a teacher can readily select the objectives, content, and instructional materials required to meet local needs.

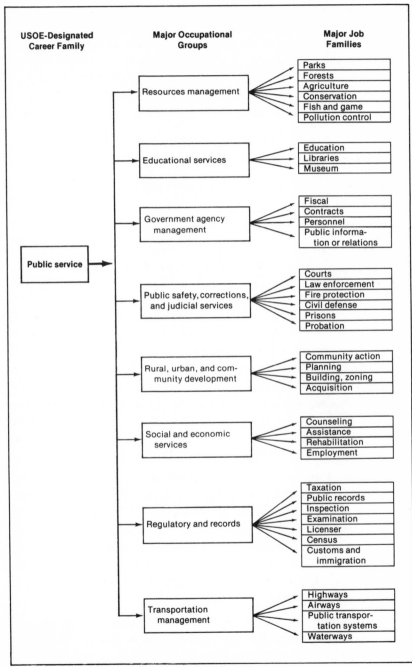

Figure 3.6. Major Civilian Occupational Groups and Job
Families in Public Service

Field Testing

The first two sets of guidelines are currently being field tested in selected high schools in California and New York. Other materials developed by the public service occupations project are oriented toward preparing for public service occupations and are scheduled for field testing. They include:

(1) Social and economic services

(2) Education services

(3) Public safety, correction, and judicial services

(4) Parks and recreational services

Enrichment of Teacher and Counselor Competencies in a Career Education Project

One of the first questions asked when elementary school career education programs are being developed is: What career development concepts should be included in a K–6 career education curriculum? In an attempt to answer the question, and also to develop appropriate materials, the above-named project, known as the ETC Project, was funded in 1972 under provisions of Part I of the vocational education amendments of 1968. The project, directed by Dr. Marla Peterson, of Eastern Illinois University, has had as its purposes the following (Peterson *et al.*, 1974, p. 2):

(1) Develop, evaluate, and disseminate career education curriculum guides that are applicable to any school with grade levels functionally equivalent to kindergarten to sixth grade and which result in the integration of positive values and attitudes toward work, self-awareness, development and decision-making skills, and awareness of occupational opportunities in career lines within major occupational fields.

(2) Develop, implement, evaluate, and disseminate sample teaching-learning modules for K–6 career education curriculum guides achieved by fusing or coordinating academic and occupational concepts and using multi-media instructional tools.

    (3) Develop, evaluate, and disseminate a design of a K–6 career education instructional system which is adaptable to any elementary instructional program and which may serve as an alternative to present career education instructional systems.

Initial efforts of the ETC Project were directed toward acquiring information. As a result of the initial efforts, the project was able to assemble and disseminate early in 1973 the publication, *A Bibliography of K–6 Career Education Materials.* A second book, *A Curriculum Design: Concepts and Components,* has recently been published by the ETC Project. In this book, the project has identified concepts that appear to be appropriate for the K–6 curriculum as they relate to the following dimensions of career development: attitudes and appreciations, career information, coping behaviors, decision making, educational awareness, life-style, and self-development. These are shown, as they in turn relate to the total K–6 curriculum, in Figure 3.7.

It is intended that the concepts presented in the second publication will serve as a blueprint for project staff members to develop teaching units and prototype student materials. It is contemplated that each teaching unit will: (1) focus on one (or in some cases, several) concepts, (2) be tied directly to a subject matter area (mathematics, language arts, science, or social studies), and (3) relate to an occupation or occupational cluster area.

Consistent with the search for meaningful definitions, the ETC Project developed the following definition of career education for its own guidance:

> Career education in the elementary school is the curriculum which results when career development concepts and subject matter concepts are brought together in an instructional system that has meaning for children.... Career development includes those concepts which are related to: attitudes and appreciations, coping behaviors, career information, decision making, educational awareness, life-style, and self-development.... Career education activities (1) emanate from the concepts that are related to the seven dimensions of career development... (2) act as syn-

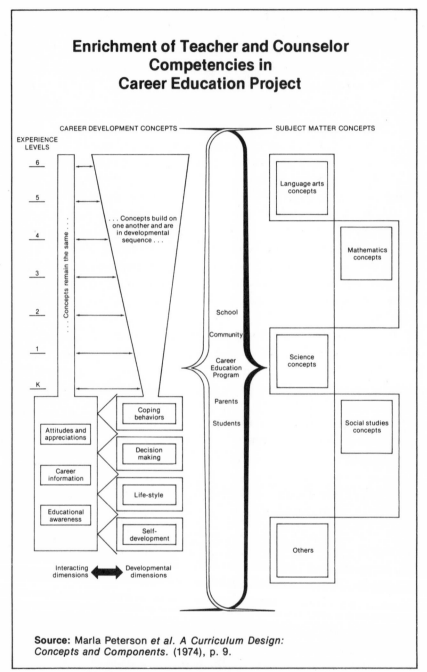

Figure 3.7. ETC Project's Career Education
Curriculum Model (K–6)

Coding	Titles
A	Photographers (BCO-GCO)
B	Illustrators (BCO-GCO)
C	Correspondents (BCO-GCO)
D	Telephone "operators" (LCO)
E	Message "assemblers" (BCO-GCO-LCO)
F	Image carrier "preparers" (GCO)
G	Image "transferrers" (GCO)
H	Finishers (GCO)
J	Telecommunications "operators" (BCO-LCO)
K	Supervisors (BCO-GCO-LCO)
M	Sales-service representatives (BCO-GCO-LCO)
N	Telecommunications "installers" (BCO-LCO)
P	Graphic equipment "installers" (GCO)

Source: W. Lee Foust *et al.,* "CMO Occupational Families"
(Corvallis, Oregon: Communications Media Occupations Cluster, 1974).
Unpublished paper.

Figure 3.8. CMO Project's Occupational Families

thesizing agents to bring subject matter concepts and career development concepts together, (3) revolve around life-based experiences, and (4) are intended for use by all students throughout their educational programs.

The materials developed by the ETC Project have been organized in terms of the seven dimensions listed earlier and are readily adaptable to all of the subject matter concepts shown in Figure 3.8.

The Communications Media Occupations Cluster Project

In yet another project operated with funds provided under Part I of the vocational education amendments of 1968, a concerted attempt has been made to create a more effective delivery system for career education efforts. In this project — the communications media occupations (CMO) project — a priority function has been to develop an information system that would provide the learner with information about the world of work. In doing so, those responsible for its development thought that decision making (by the learner) will be made more effective, regardless of specific level — i.e., awareness, orientation, or in-depth exploration level.

Once a learner has made a decision concerning a particular career, a new set of informational needs becomes apparent. At this point, the learner needs indicators of the occupations, educational requirements, and training opportunities that are available. And institutional program planners responsible for designing programs need to know more than just the number of learners interested in receiving training in a given occupational area. Information as to the employment potential at the national, regional, state, and local levels, as well as the number of workers presently available or training, is of great value to both the learner and the institutional program planner.

Field Test Information System

Toward these ends the CMO project, under direction of Dr. Lee Foust, Jr., and located at Oregon State University, has developed a prototypical information system for use with the communications media occupations cluster. The system was developed in cooperation with personnel responsible for a similar system — the Oregon Board of Education Career Program Planning System. These two information systems share program format and were at this writing jointly operational on the Oregon State University computer system. They represent an initial reponse to the information needs described earlier. Other career education information needs exist, and it is the intent of the CMO project staff, in cooperation with Oregon Board of Education personnel, to continue to develop information systems that could serve career education needs at the national, state, or local level.

CMO Occupational Families

While the CMO project has devoted considerable attention to developmental efforts related to the information system described above, it has also been actively involved in the development of materials that could be used within the information system. Initially, the project staff divided the communications media cluster into three major areas: (1) broadcast communications occupations (BCO), (2) graphic communications occupations (GCO), and (3) line communications occupations (LCO). This in turn has led to the identification of a series of CMO occupational families. These "families," which may be found in any or all of the three major areas (BCO-GCO-LCO), are shown in Figure 3.8.

For each of the CMO occupational families, the project has developed an information base for use in the information system discussed in the preceding section. An example is shown in Figure 3.9. As can be seen in the figure, the user of the information — student, teacher, counselor, or program planner — can at a glance obtain considerable information relating to the job title having the highest employment potential and can quickly locate references to other job titles included in the family.

Field Testing

The materials that have been developed by the communications media occupations cluster project are currently being field tested in selected school systems in several western states. The computerized program, while still being tested and modified, is operational at the present time. At this writing, the project materials have not been published for distribution. It is anticipated that publication and wide distribution will be accomplished when the field testing program is completed.

The Project: Developing Career Awareness for Spanish-Surnamed People

This project, directed by Dr. Suzette Gebolys, of Central Texas College, represents still another approach used in the curriculum development projects funded under provisions of Part I of the vocational education amendments of 1968. In this project, multimedia instructional support materials were developed by the research and development division of Central Texas College and field tested in one of the Dallas middle schools.

Occupational Family: Photographers (A)   Broadcast
                                               Graphic

WTG Page: 230

The occupational family — photographers (a) — offers
employment opportunity in the broadcast and graphic
communications occupational areas. The primary occupation — high employment potential job title — is:

DOT Job Title   WTG Page   DOT Number

Photographer, News 230 143062038

The job titles in this occupational family involve the
use of photography as a technology using light to *select a
design for the production of the message* that is to be
distributed via the broadcast and graphic communications distribution systems. These job titles all require
graduation from high school. An additional year or two of
post-high school training and two to four years of
experience are required for most job titles in this occupational family. For specific information on any job title,
refer to the GED and SVP levels of education, training,
and experience provided in the alphabetical list of CMO
job titles at the end of this *Guide.*

Other CMO job titles in this occupational family are found
on:

WTG Page 230   DOT Number

Camera operator 143062010
Photographer apprentice, commercial 143062026
Photographer 143062034
Screen reported 143062046

Figure 3.9. Example of the CMO Project's Occupational Family

The materials, which included color videotape cassettes and computer-assisted instructional lessons, were designed to assist underachieving middle school students in mastering fundamental concepts of career education. In this particular effort no attempt was made to focus on specific job or occupational clusters; instead, the materials were designed to introduce the student to the world of work and at the same time enhance the self-concept of the learner.

Project Objectives and Procedures

The basic purpose of the project has already been noted. In keeping with the purpose, the project had as its objective the development and evaluation of multimedia materials focusing on career education concepts uniquely applicable to chicano students. Stated in more specific fashion, the project attempted to investigate the issue: Is there a difference in learning and attitude between subjects of different ethnic backgrounds when career education instruction is conducted via videotape cassettes and reinforced with alternating computer-assisted instructional segments?

To accomplish the objective, the project developed fifteen color videotapes and fifteen computer-assisted lessons designed specifically for use with chicano students. Thus a corollary issue to be investigated was: Are the videotape cassettes and computer-assisted lessons in career education concepts uniquely well suited to chicano students, or do all students profit equally from this experience?

The videotape cassettes and computer-assisted materials were incorporated as instructional support for a one-semester course in occupational information for eighth grade students. The materials, presented to the students as shown in Figure 3.10, served to augment regular classroom instruction.

Conclusions

The project has been completed and the results have been fully tabulated in a final report. The conclusions drawn from the effort, however, are included here in summary form:

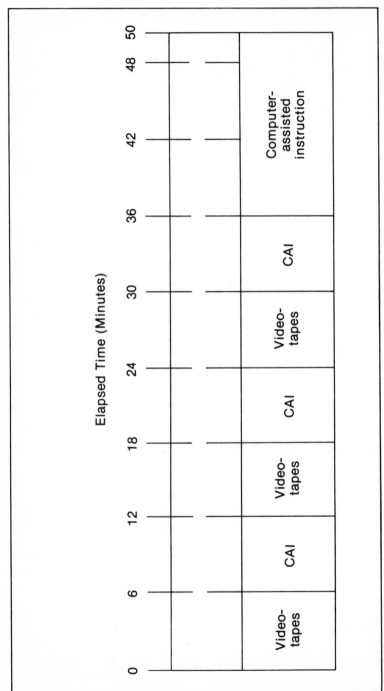

Figure 3.10. Sequence of Learning Experiences, Using Videotape Cassettes and Computer-Assisted Instructional Segments

(1) Student learning increased when classroom instruction was augmented with multimedia materials developed in this project.

(2) Increases in student learning, as measured by correct completion of the computer-assisted materials, were evenly distributed among black, chicano, and white students.

(3) Increases in student learning, as measured by the pre- and post-test, were greatest for black females; all students in the treatment group, however, averaged a higher score on the post-test than did those in the control group.

(4) Student motivation, as measured by class attendance, was higher for those participants in the treatment group.

(5) Students positively responded to questionnaire items dealing with their reactions to the experience. While chicano students reported more difficulty in understanding the videotapes and the computer-assisted instructions than did the black students, this is partially explained by the general English language problems experienced by these students.

(6) The computer-assisted lessons were found to be a usable instructional tool for students with below-average reading levels. The individualized nature of these lessons permitted the students to progress at their own pace, thus accommodating their slow reading comprehension rates.

(7) Students evidenced a great deal of enthusiasm and interest to the total experience, particularly to the immediate personal feedback provided in the computer-assisted lessons.

Summary

The curriculum development projects that have been described constitute only a portion of those which have been funded under provisions of Part I of the vocational education amendments of 1968. Those that have been described were chosen only to illustrate the variety of approaches that have been taken. In one approach the focus was on the development of content material, while in another it was on concepts. In still another approach the emphasis was on the development and use of technology-based information systems; and in yet another emphasis was on the unique blending of technology and content for use with minority and culturally disadvantaged students.

As the products of these and other projects become available, teachers, coordinators, supervisors, and directors will find their resources for career education greatly enhanced. Both state and local education agencies will have available many more tools—all designed to ensure that career education, in its most meaningful form, does reach the student and does make a difference.

Use of Career Education Curriculum Materials

As indicated earlier in this chapter, there has been some reluctance to define career education in precise terms. Because of this, some state and local education agencies may perceive that career education curriculum materials developed with the help of national or federal agencies conflict to some extent with their own existing educational philosophy. This, however, should not be a serious problem if the materials that have been developed are adaptable to state and local needs.

Many state and local education agencies, in trying to help career education practitioners cope with all of the problems they face, have developed criteria to determine the acceptability of curriculum materials. Some of these criteria are in the form of checklists that can be used to evaluate the worth of specific curriculum modifications. One such checklist has been prepared by and used in the Ohio career development program (illustrated in Figure 3.11). As is evident, the checklist is designed to assist personnel from both state and local levels in examining curricular materials with some degree of objectivity and specificity. In addition, the checklist might also be used

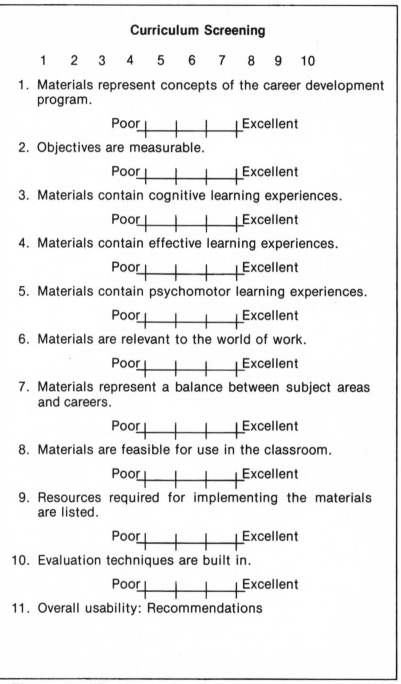

Figure 3.11. Checklist for Ohio's Career Development Program

effectively by citizens' study or advisory committees as they work with educational personnel.

In some states, the criteria for assessing components of career education – including curricular developments – are presented in the form of guidelines, position statements, or conceptual models. The Nevada State Department of Education, for example, has prepared and distributed a monograph, *Career Development in Nevada*, which contains both a policy and position statement and a conceptual model. The monograph is intended as a resource tool that can be used by local school personnel as they develop and implement programs of career education and, by inference, to evaluate the degree to which programs and materials achieve the purposes that have been assigned.

Barriers to the Use of Curricular Materials

Ordinarily, philosophies toward career education do not vary substantially from state to state or from district to district. The differences that do exist would appear to be more in terminology than in substance. However, even differences in terminology – or more accurately, differences in *understandings* of terminology – may well be a reason for either nonacceptance or outright rejection of a given curricular approach in career education. In addition, it should be noted that in recent years there has developed in many state and local education agencies a sizable cadre of educators who are quite knowledgeable in the skills of curriculum development. Such educators may perceive their own product to be superior to a "ready-made" one.

If career education is to be a moving force in American education, every effort must be made to achieve the commonality of understanding that is needed. At the same time, every effort must also be made to use the best procedures and materials that are avialable, regardless of who produced them. And if it is apparent that the "best of two worlds" should be used, then so be it – as Hoyt (1974) and his colleagues have implied:

> It is apparent that, at present, most development of career education instructional materials goes on in isolation from similar efforts in other school systems.

> It is also apparent that the most innovative materials, at present, are being developed at the local school system level and not in the college and university settings. . . . What is really needed, however, is the availability of reasonable effective materials which can be *revised* by classroom teachers. (Emphasis added.)

However, the ability or expertise needed to adapt, revise, or construct curricular materials is not all that is needed if state and local education agencies are to use, either *in toto* of in part, the curricular materials that have been developed. Some general guidelines or criteria are also needed. Four such guidelines were developed by the American Institutes of Research in the Behavioral Sciences. According to the Institutes, curricular materials for career education should be:

(1) *Economically feasible:* The cost of implementation must not be too high for typical school systems. It must fit within the confines of normal school expenditures for textbooks, workbooks, routine instructional materials, and classroom operation costs.

(2) *Predicated upon regular classroom staffing patterns:* Long-term in-service teacher training, extensive use of teacher aides or paraprofessionals, or the use of new categories of technical specialists is neither characteristic of most public education nor likely to be characteristic in the immediately foreseeable future.

(3) *Contained within the current allocation of teacher time and effort:* It cannot be expected either to extend the school day or to supplant present parts of the curriculum.

(4) *Amenable to local needs, interests and options.* It is unrealistic to assume that fixed "canned" or "prepackaged" curriculums can anticipate all possible combinations of state, local, and personal needs. Options for selective access and use, based upon local district and learner needs, must be provided in the curriculum design and structure.

Thus with the commitment of federal, state, and local personnel to develop sound curricular materials in career education, it appears that all efforts will further ensure that career education is a movement which reaches beyond administrative doors into the classroom for the improvement of education for each student.

Selected References

Dunn, James; *et al. A Curriculum Design and Instructional Objective Catalog.* Palo Alto, California: American Institutes for Research in the Behavioral Sciences. 1973.

Foust, W. Lee; *et al.* "CMO Occupational Families." Corvallis, Oregon: Communications Media Occupations Cluster Project. 1973. Mimeographed.

Hoyt, Kenneth B.; *et al. Career Education: What It Is and How to Do It.* Second edition. Salt Lake City: Olympus Publishing Company. 1974.

Morgan, Robert; *et al.* Editors. *Synopses of Selected Career Education: A National Overview of Career Education.* Raleigh: North Carolina State University, National Center for Occupational Education. 1972.

_____; *et al.* Editors. *An Anthology of Fifteen Career Education Programs.* Raleigh: North Carolina State University, Center for Occupational Education. 1973.

North Carolina Career Education Task Force. *Career Education: A Report of the North Carolina Career Education Task Force.* Raleigh: North Carolina State Department of Public Instruction. 1973.

Ohio State University. *Career Education Curriculum Materials: Preliminary Products List.* Columbus: Ohio State University, Center for Vocational and Technical Education. 1973.

_____. "Developmental Program Goals for the Comprehensive Career Education Model." Columbus: Ohio State University, Center for Vocational and Technical Education. 1972. Mimeographed.

_____. *Staff Development Products.* Columbus: Ohio State University, Center for Vocational and Technical Education. 1973.

Page, Jean. *Career Education in New Mexico: Implementation Guidelines.* Santa Fe: New Mexico State Department of Education. 1973.

Peterson, Marla; *et al. A Bibiliography of K-6 Career Education Materials.* Charleston: Eastern Illinois University, Center for Educational Studies. 1973.

_____; *et al. A Curriculum Design: Concepts and Components.* Charleston: Eastern Illinois University, Center for Educational Studies. 1974.

U.S. Department of Labor. *Dictionary of Occupational Titles.* Washington, D.C.: U.S. Government Printing Office. Various years.

Weagraff, Patrick; *et al. Public Service Occupations in Career Education.* Sacramento: California State Department of Education, Division of Vocational Education. 1973.

_____; *et al. Preparing for Public Service Occupations: Common Core.* Sacramento: California State Department of Education, Division of Vocational Education. 1973.

4

Models, Elements, and Characteristics of Career Education

David L. Jesser
Byron Vanier*

For some time, numerous education agencies at every level of education have been seriously involved in a comprehensive examination or study of the concept of career education. State, local, post-secondary, and national education agencies and institutions have all engaged in a process of sorting out the many definitions, components, and purposes of career education that have been formulated during the past few years. At the same time, these agencies have also engaged in a process of revising, refining, modifying, or otherwise adapting these definitions, components, and purposes in the hope that the end product will better, or more nearly, meet individual agency needs. As a result, there are countless "models" of career education, and to some the multitude of models seemingly approaches chaos. However, such is not the case.

While educators and proponents of career education will readily recognize that a variety of individual approaches exists, together with a wide range of individual differences, those same educators and proponents of career education must also recognize that while the approaches differ in specific detail, there are basic similarities — threads of commonality — to be found in each.

---

*Formerly with the Nebraska State Department of Education.

For example, one of the fundamental purposes of career education is that the educational program at every level be relevant to the total world of work, to the community, and to society in general. It is difficult to identify any model that does not recognize, in some fashion, this purpose. Another basic purpose of career education consists of helping leaders understand more about themselves, the world of work, and how they relate to it. Again, virtually all models recognize this. And still another basic purpose consists of helping every learner (from kindergarten on) become better prepared to choose, in a rational manner, a career field that will enable the person to be a productive, contributing member of society and live a completely self-rewarding life. Once again, most models recognize this purpose.

The broad kinds of similarities of the basic purposes serve also to illustrate the reasons for the common characteristics that are found in most of the models that have been developed for career education. Several of these models are examined in this chapter. If we look at them in some detail, it may be possible to generate still another model—one designed to more adequately meet the educational needs of a state education agency, a local school system, or an institution of higher learning. And by more adequately meeting those needs, we can better serve the needs of the individual learner.

Career Education Models

As the concept of career education has evolved or developed, some programs that have been generated have attempted to incorporate career education concepts into every subject area in the curriculum. Examples of this approach were discussed in a preceding chapter and need not be repeated here. It should be noted, however, that other programs have emerged which include only resource units in a limited number of subject areas, and these only at certain grade levels. These approaches are obviously very different. Basically, however, in the programs of both approaches the terms "career awareness," "career exploration," and "career preparation" are to be frequently found. In this vein, these or similar terms are readily noticeable in the various models of career education.

U.S. Office of Education Model

When Dr. Marland first discussed the need for programs in career education, he envisaged an educational program in which elementary students would be helped to understand more about the wide range of jobs in our society, together with the roles and requirements that exist in and among them. He envisaged a program in which junior high school students would be able to explore, through hands-on experiences, a limited number of occupational fields or clusters. And he discussed the need for a program in which every senior high school student would have an opportunity to become prepared for employment upon exiting from high school or for entry into some form of post-secondary education.

The USOE model, as shown in Figure 4.1, contains the basic characteristics or components that have already been mentioned. Provision is made for students to become acquainted with the world of work and their relationship to it; provision is also made for students to have opportunities to explore broad occupational areas. And, as the model shows, students are given the opportunity either to acquire entry skills for specific occupations or to acquire the skills needed for them to move into the next preparational level.

For example, if a student were to choose to exit at grade ten, certain basic job-entry skills would have been acquired, thus enabling the student to enter the world of work. Or, as the model indicates, a student exiting at grade twelve should be able to enter a specialized occupation or enter into a period of more specialized education. Exit from the latter should be into a more technical occupation or another period of specialized education. The several components are explained more fully in the following discussion.

Awareness Stage

The USOE model includes kindergarten through sixth grade in the "career awareness stage." Students in these grades should become aware of the world of work and the wide range of occupations that exist within it; and they should understand how they themselves relate to the world of work. Since the model was developed, there have been numerous attempts by

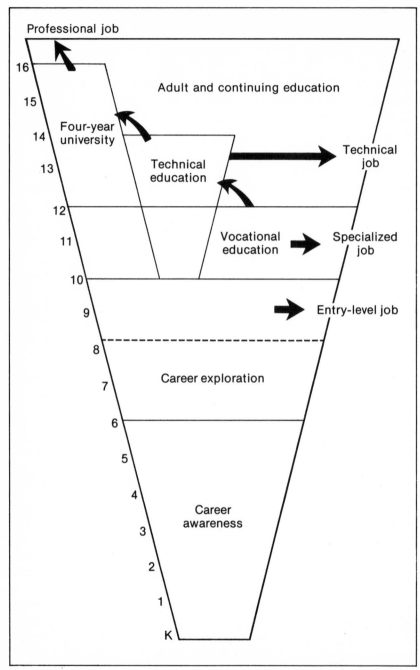

Figure 4.1. U.S. Office of Education's Career
Education Model

state and local education agencies and other advocates of career education to refine it or further delineate or define it. For example, the Portland, Oregon, career development program (Rasmussen and Carpenter, 1971) contains — for this level of career education — an "orientation to occupations" segment that is designed to enable students to:

(1) Learn attitudes of respect and appreciation for all types of work and for workers in all fields

(2) Relate the subject matter of each discipline to occupations

(3) Express their own interests, aptitudes, and abilities in several of the major career fields

(4) Make tentative choices of career fields that they would like to explore

(5) Know the wide range of occupations open to them

In similar fashion, the Oregon career education program — "The Oregon Way" — lists the following as the career awareness phase, which includes programs in the elementary grades where the students will:

(1) Develop awareness of the many occupational careers available

(2) Develop awareness of self in relation to the occupational career role

(3) Develop foundations for wholesome attitudes toward work and society

(4) Develop attitudes of respect and appreciation toward workers in all fields

(5) Make tentative choices of career clusters to explore in greater depth during middle school years

Goldhammer and Taylor (1972) suggest that the awareness stage should provide for five major functions to be fulfilled:

(1) Basic skills of learning and social development

(2) Examination of essential functions pertaining to life and the individual and social activities of human beings

(3) Examination of the basic characteristics of a person's life in various societies

(4) Exploration of the environment and nature and how humans learned about them and used them

(5) Exploration of basic interests and potentialities of each child

These examples reflect both the manner in which similarities exist and the way in which individual modifications might be made. In this context, these should suffice; however, they should simultaneously provide sound guidelines to the interested and concerned educator who is trying to refine or redefine a local program.

Marla Peterson and her associates in the Enrichment of Teacher-Counselor Competencies project include basic concepts that children in kindergarten through sixth grade should be aided in learning. These concepts are catalogued as to the affective, cognitive, or psychomotor domain and are presented in terms of six readiness levels.

Career Exploration Stage

In referring once again to the USOE model in Figure 4.1, we note that grades seven through nine are included in the "career exploration stage," where it is intended that students be given an opportunity to explore in depth their chosen occupational families. Such exploration may consist of hands-on experiences, field trips, contact with resource people from business and industry, or observational activities related to occupational clusters.

To again illustrate how different yet similar approaches have occurred, let us examine Portland's career development program, which includes an occupational exploration phase that consists of a variety of exploratory experiences of sufficient scope and depth to enable students to:

(1) Understand the physical, educational, and skill requirements of typical occupations

(2) Relate their own interests, aptitudes, and abilities to the requirements of typical occupations in a number of career clusters

(3) Appreciate the importance of education and career training as preparation for a satisfying life

(4) Arrive at a tentative career choice in an appropriate field

At the state level, many state education agencies have either adapted or redefined the career exploration stage as found in the USOE model. The Oregon Board of Education, for example, has included in its plan, "The Oregon Way," a career exploration program for middle school years, usually grades six or seven through ten, where students will:

(1) Explore key occupational areas and assess their own interests and abilities

(2) Become familiar with occupational classifications and clusters

(3) Develop awareness of relevant factors to be considered in decision making

(4) Gain experience in meaningful decision making

(5) Develop tentative occupational plans and arrive at a tentative career choice

Goldhammer and Taylor (1972) suggest several functions with which career education programs in the middle or junior high school years should be concerned:

(1) Continued growth and increased competence in the use of basic skills

(2) Examination of a broad range of vocational, avocational, family life, citizenship, and cultural career alternatives

(3) Exploration of several potential personal career opportunities

(4) Development of skills and attitudes toward career choices

(5) Preliminary selection of general areas for future vocational careers

(6) Broadened knowledge of personal and educational requirements involved in various careers

(7) Examination of humankind's value and belief systems

As the USOE model and other representative models (to be discussed subsequently) indicate, career education consists of a *total sequence* of activities — not of several unrelated parts. Thus it would be fallacy to think that any one segment shown in the upcoming models is more or less important than any other, for no segment can properly function in the absence of the others. But while all segments are important to the total process, it must be recognized that as the learner progresses through the sequence, the career exploration stage is the pivotal point because it is during this stage that the learner begins to narrow career choices and to focus more clearly on areas of preparation. It is vital, then, that career education practitioners and program planners ensure that during the middle or junior high school years, students are aware that this segment is truly significant and not just something tossed in to fill up the hiatus between elementary school and high school.

Career Preparation Stage

Within the USOE career education model, grades ten through twelve are included in the "career preparation stage." During this time, students are given the opportunity to acquire the necessary entry-level competencies in their (tentatively) chosen occupational field or to become prepared to enter some form of post-secondary educational program. In the Portland program, this stage is termed "occupational preparation," and is described as consisting of programs that, according to Rasmussen and Carpenter (1971), "provide students with in-depth instruction in occupational skills and knowledge sufficient for effective job entry or advanced occupational training." Occupational preparation programs, in the Portland approach, should enable students to:

(1) Perform the tasks basic to one or more occupations to standards of accuracy and speed that will qualify them for employment in an entry-level job

(2) Refine or confirm their tentative career choices

(3) Acquire occupational skills, knowledge, and understanding sufficient to appreciate the need for and to

pursue more advanced occupational training on a full-
or part-time basis

(4) Learn *acceptable job attitudes* and appreciate the importance of their occupation and standards

Oregon's state education agency (the state's Board of Education) has indicated that the occupational stage should be
centered on career cluster programs in eleventh and twelfth
grades, where students will:

(1) Acquire occupational skills and knowledge for entry-
level employment or advanced occupational training

(2) Tie a majority of high school experiences into generalized career goals

(3) Develop acceptable job habits

(4) Be involved in cooperative work experiences and have
an opportunity to be a member of a vocational youth
organization

Goldhammer and Taylor (1972) outline several major functions of the senior high school (which they see as tenth through
twelfth grades):

(1) Emphasis on continuous refinement, use, and application of basic skills

(2) Development of specific knowledge and skills needed
for family life, avocational, citizenship, and cultural
careers

(3) Exploration and personal testing of avocational career
opportunities within the specific cluster or area

(4) Selection of specific career and initial preparation and
exploration of post-high school preparation potentials

(5) Development of some salable skills

These should also be valuable both to career education planners and to program personnel.

Post-secondary Stage

The USOE model is not only directed toward students from
kindergarten through twelfth grade, it also includes those who

will be exiting school and entering the world of work. This in no way implies lack of concern for those who will have additional schooling, for a student may exit secondary school and still participate in a technical education program, a four-year college or university, or some other academic or military form of education. In any case, it should be obvious that success in a post-secondary program will be predicated upon the totality (and degree of success) of the preceding K–12 program.

Elements of career awareness, exploration, and preparation also exist in the adult phase of the program, with basic differences of philosophy. Adult programs rest upon an individual's previous experiences and activities that were meaningful, whereas the K–12 program develops these experiences and activities. It is also essential that adults have flexibility in entry and exit of the program so that their needs are better served. The adult phase of career education holds the promise of making the time-honored expression "lifelong learning" a reality in our technologically oriented society.

In the Oregon approach, the post-secondary effort is called "occupational specialization" – an apt description. It includes programs in community colleges, apprenticeships, vocational and technical schools, and four-year colleges and universities. Within this framework, Oregon's learners were to:

(1) Be involved in developing specific occupational knowledge and preparation in a specialized job area

(2) Have the opportunity to form meaningful employer-employee types of relationships

(3) Be provided necessary retraining or upgrading skills

Other Models

Among educators, someone once said, there is a "semantic looseness." Although this may be true throughout education, it is indeed a truism in career education. We have discussed the many kinds of concepts; and as it was with these, so it is with models. In some instances, they are perceived as being miniature, scaled-down replicas, exact in every detail, of some object. In other instances, they are used to portray in some fashion ideas, concepts, procedures, systems, and the like.

The USOE model gave us both a procedure and a system in which career education might be incorporated into a total education system. Those described in this section give similar ideas and procedures on how career education "fits" into the total education system. No one model for career education is likely to provide all of the answers to given situations. There will always be unique circumstances, and these will require adaptation or modification of the basic models. Those presented here serve to assist educators who are to be the practitioners of career education in perceiving ways in which models — designed to meet needs unique to each situation — may be created.

The Oregon Model

In many respects, the Oregon model (Figure 4.2) is like the USOE model, for they both are in pyramid form (albeit, one is inverted) — each showing the progression of the student through the school years of career education. While the USOE model seems to portray a constant broadening of learner options, the Oregon model portrays a movement — in a series of decision-making points — that lead to refinement and specialization as the learner proceeds through the sequence. Both concepts (broadening and movement) are major goals of career education. The significance of guidance and counseling is stressed in the Oregon model.

The Nevada Model

While several state education agencies have developed models similar to the vertical schematic used in Oregon, others, during their own process of "sorting out," have depicted career education in many different ways. The Nevada State Department of Education, for example, has developed a series of Venn diagram-type conceptualizations to portray career education. The first of these, shown in chapter 1 (Figure 1.2), is intended to focus on the learner within the "real" world. The model illustrates that the four learning environments (school, home, community, and workplace) not only interrelate, they are in fact dependent upon one another.

For purposes of clarification, the Nevada State Department of Education has included the following definitions for use with Figure 1.2:

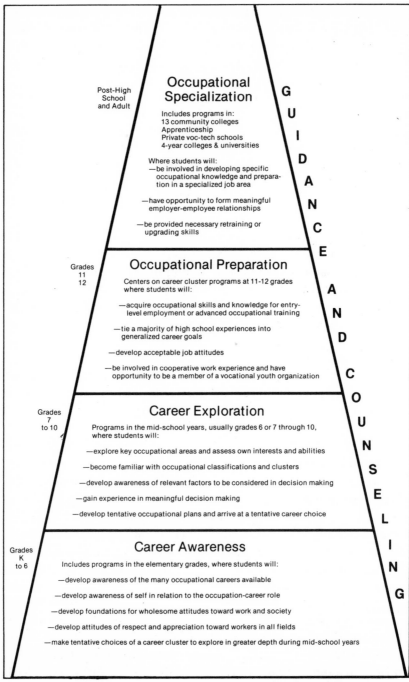

Figure 4.2. Career Education — The Oregon Way

(1) *Real world:* The universe of human experience affecting individual life-styles; everything that contributes to human development

(2) *Workplace:* The areas where one performs labor, tasks, or duties which afford people their accustomed means of livelihood or results in personal satisfaction

(3) *Community:* An interacting population of various kinds of individuals in a common location, linked by common rules, laws, or values

(4) *Home:* A place where a person lives, either alone or with others

(5) *School:* A place for formalized teaching of persons through a series of structured experiences

(6) *Learner:* Any person

Two companion diagrams, also developed by the Nevada State Department of Education for use in its career education effort, are shown in Figures 4.3 and 4.4. The former is intended to illustrate the interrelationship of experiences, occupations, and subject matter areas in the educational arena, while the latter is intended to depict the several stages of career education.

The Ohio Model

In Ohio, the career education effort is described in terms of career development, and the model that has been developed by personnel in the Ohio state education agency to depict career education is termed "Ohio's Career Development Continuum." The Ohio model is illustrated in Figure 4.5, and, as will be noted, portrays the process of career education in a linear (horizontal) fashion, proceeding from kindergarten through the post-secondary (adult) years.

The Ohio career development program (career motivation, orientation, and exploration) is intended for all students in kindergarten through tenth grade. At grade nine, as the model indicates, some students become involved in an "occupational work adjustment program," while others may participate in an "occupational laboratory." In grades eleven and twelve, students participate in programs designed to equip them with job-

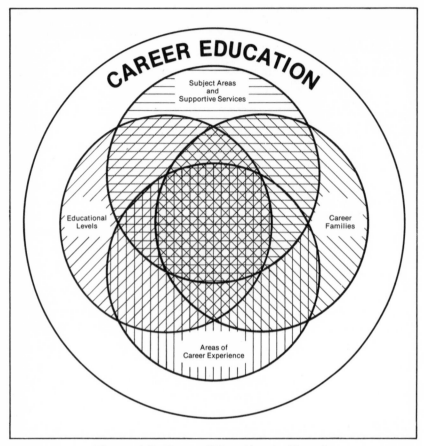

Figure 4.3. Career Education in Nevada

entry skills, necessary requirements for specialized training, or those requisites needed for college entrance.

The Michigan Model

In Michigan, the concept and process of career education has been depicted (and labeled) as a "Tree Model of Career Education." This is illustrated in Figure 4.6, and portrays the "in-school" components of career education (self-awareness, career awareness and planning, and academic and vocational education) as the roots of a tree. The trunk is related to occupations, while the branches (life roles) are supported by "continuous education." The Michigan State Department of

Education has also developed a chart, or model, in which the components of career education are depicted as shown in Figure 4.7.

The Mississippi Model

In Mississippi, a model for career education has been developed not only to show the sequence of activities in which the learner would be involved, but also to show the emphases, methods, and techniques considered to be necessary in leading the learner to a rewarding life role. The Mississippi model, illustrated in Figure 4.8, also portrays the several avenues open to learners, before as well as after graduation from high school. All of the avenues lead eventually into the world of work.

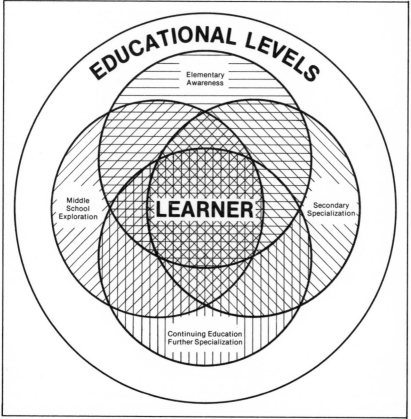

Figure 4.4. Educational Levels and Career Education in Nevada

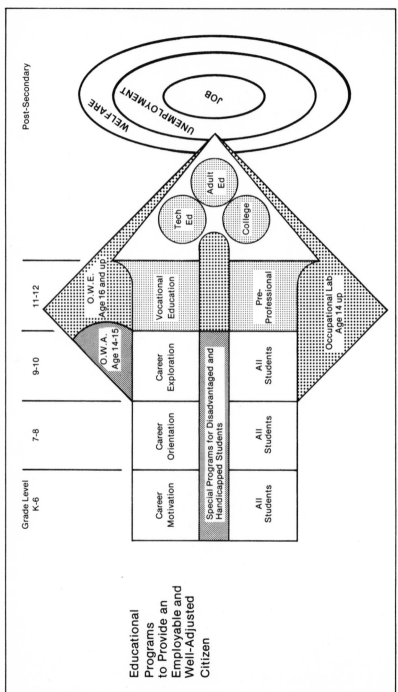

Figure 4.5. Ohio's Career Development Continuum

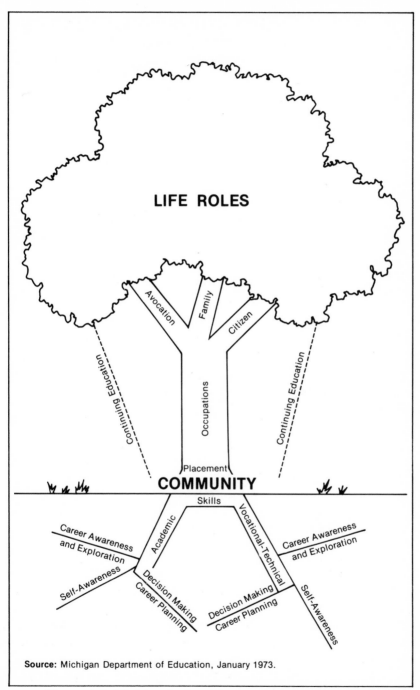

Source: Michigan Department of Education, January 1973.

Figure 4.6. Michigan's Tree Model of Career Education

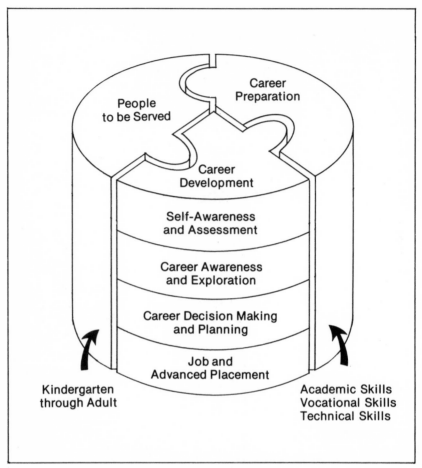

Figure 4.7. Michigan's Conceptual Model of the Components of Career Education

The Wisconsin Model

For Wisconsin's concept of career education, the state's Department of Instruction created a three-sided model (Figure 4.9). The key elements (one at each angle) are (1) self, (2) career planning and preparation, and (3) the world of work. As the figure illustrates, the relationships among the key elements must be considered in the process of career development. Also, it shows that there is — during the process — an "emerging self" with some kind of "vocational identity." This emerging self will, through rational decision making, cause

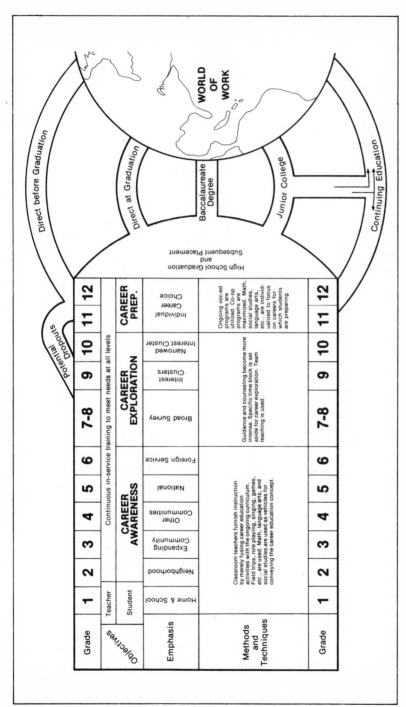

Figure 4.8. Mississippi's Conceptual Model of Career Education (K-12)

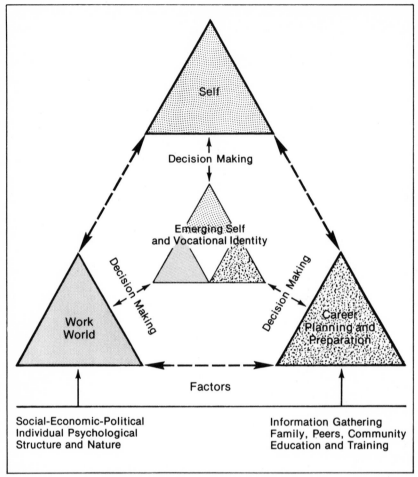

Figure 4.9. Wisconsin's Triangular
Career Development Model

other relationships with the key elements to emerge. The definition given to "self" is: "How one person perceives himself in
relation to his individual characteristics and the relationships
he has with others within his intervening environment."

The Kansas Model

In Kansas, the concept of career education is perceived as
being a developmental process — one that begins with a formal
educational program (kindergarten) and extends through the
adult years into the retirement years (Figure 4.10). The model

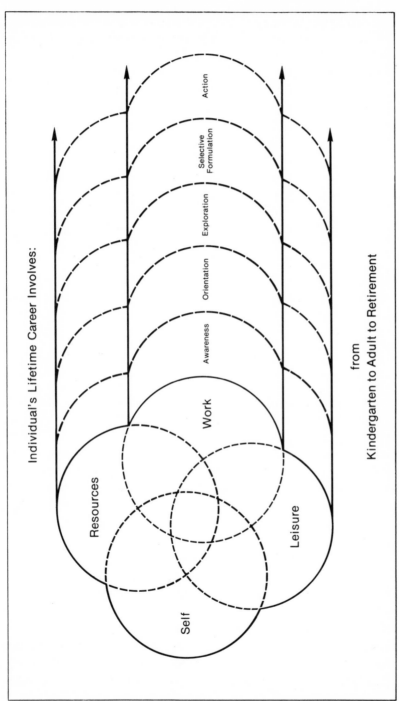

Figure 4.10. Kansas' Conceptual Model for Developmental Career Education

graphically indicates that an individual's lifetime career involves four closely related components: (1) self, (2) resources, (3) work, and (4) leisure. For each of the components, the process of career education will lead the individual from awareness to action. More importantly, the model shows that through the process, the several interrelationships should be constantly considered.

The Georgia Model

While the Georgia model shown in Figures 4.11 and 4.12 does not look like the models previously discussed, it does illustrate a system for career education. As shown in the first model, the necessary elements of career education are placed along one axis, while the various learner levels are placed along the other. This grid can then be used to identify where particular activities should occur. In the chart in Figure 4.12, the various blocks in the grid have been filled in with suggestions on *which* activity is to be done ("programs") and suggestions on *who* ("staff") is to be responsible for the particular activity.

The Alabama Model

The Alabama model is constructed in still another manner. It shows a continuum from kindergarten through twelfth grade (Figure 4.13), and also shows the basic elements of career education and what each element is intended to produce. This model, as did others, takes the child from the self-awareness stage to "self" and "social fulfillment." In the center column is shown the elements (influences) that surround the child as he or she continues through the career education process.

The Louisiana Model

The model for career education that was developed for use in Louisiana (Figure 4.14) is a sequential plan. The several stages, or elements, of career education are indicated. The model also includes the process needed for each of the six stages depicted. Information and experience, the figure shows, will lead to self-development, which in turn will lead to individual success in each stage — with the extra bonus of a healthy sense of well-being.

Elements	(K-6) Childhood	(7-9) Early Adolescent	(10-12) Adolescent	(13-14) Late Adolescent	Adult
1 — Orientation					
2 — Exploration					
3 — Interdisciplinary					
4 — Career curriculum	▓	▓			
5 — Outreach	▓	▓			
6 — Intensive short-term specialized courses	▓	▓			
7 — Placement and follow through	▓	▓			
8 — Guidance and counseling					

Figure 4.11. Georgia's Model Depicting Levels at Which Elements of a Career Development Program Are Necessary

Programs	(K-6) Childhood	(7-9) Early Adolescent	(10-12) Adolescent	(13-14) Late Adolescent	Adult
Orientation	1 a c	6 a c / 2 3 4 b	5 b or c / 7 a e 6 a	6 a 5 c / 8 e e a	5 c
Exploration	1 a c	6 a c / 2 3 4 b	5 b or c / 7 a e 6 a	6 a 5 c / 8 e e a	5 c 8 e
Interdisciplinary	1 a c	2 3 4 a b	7 a e	8 e a	8 a e
Career curriculum			7 d or e	8 d or e	8 d or e
Outreach			b c or d	b c or d	b c or d
Intensive short-term specialized courses			b d e 9 c	b d or / e 9 c	b d or e / 9 c
Placement and follow through			b or c	c or b	c b
Guidance and counseling	6 c	6 c	5 c 6 c	5 c 6 c	5 c 6 c

Programs
1 — World of work curriculum
2 — Across-the-board exploratory program
3 — Mini-exploratory courses (quarter length)
4 — One-year exploratory courses
5 — Career decision-making and planning courses
6 — Fuse career activities into each curriculum cluster
7 — Career curriculum
8 — Occupational career curriculum
9 — Supportive and monitoring counseling

Staff
a — Regular teachers (general and academic)
b — Specialized staff (exploratory and others)
c — Guidance counselor
d — Cooperative teacher
e — Job preparatory teachers

Figure 4.12. Georgia's Model for Staff and Program Implementation

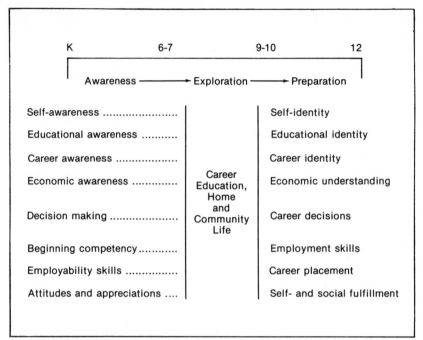

Figure 4.13. Alabama's Elements of Career Education

Summary

We have attempted to illustrate, with the help of career education models of various states, how the concept of career education has been interpreted by educators and lay citizens in selected states. The USOE model gave us an insight into how this concept is viewed at the national level. The similarities and yet differences were indeed noticeable. (We hasten to add that differences are attributable to the fact that local and state statutes, regulations, policies, or interpretations of need are often the determining factor that creates these differences.) Yet it is readily evident that a *process* for career education has been established by these states and contains the basic elements: awareness, exploration, and preparation.

Instructional Models for Career Education

Process and content models have been described above and curriculum models were discussed in chapter 3. We now turn our attention to how – in what instructional mode – career education might best be presented to the learners. For this purpose, USOE has developed four models, through research and development activities, which are intended to facilitate career education goals. In August 1972, these models were transferred to the National Institute of Education, since most of the research and development responsibilities were to be given to this new agency. The models were originally conceived of as a tool to: (1) investigate and test alternative hypotheses on the delivery of career education, and (2) design and develop prototypical career education programs congruent with each of the various hypotheses.

Model I: School-Based Career Education

In the school-based model of career education, the intent was to develop a system in which learning experiences would be more relevant and meaningful for the learner. To accomplish this purpose, designers of the system realized that learning experiences must be closely related to the objectives of career education – meaning that fundamental changes would be needed in the curriculums of public schools. Ohio State University's Center for Vocational and Technical Education had the responsibility of developing the school-based career education model.

In 1971, the Center contracted with six local school systems throughout the nation to further develop (and infuse into their educational programs) a comprehensive career education model. These six school systems – Atlanta (Georgia), Hackensack (New Jersey), Jefferson County (Colorado), Los Angeles (California), Mesa (Arizona), and Pontiac (Michigan) – were to engage in what was perceived to be a five-year, four-stage effort.

The objectives of the school-based career education model were that an education system would be developed and tested which would develop in students:

(1) A comprehensive awareness of career options

(2) A concept of self in keeping with a work-oriented society, including positive attitudes about work, school,

and society, and a sense of satisfaction resulting from successful experiences in these areas

(3) Personal characteristics such as self-respect, initiative, and resourcefulness

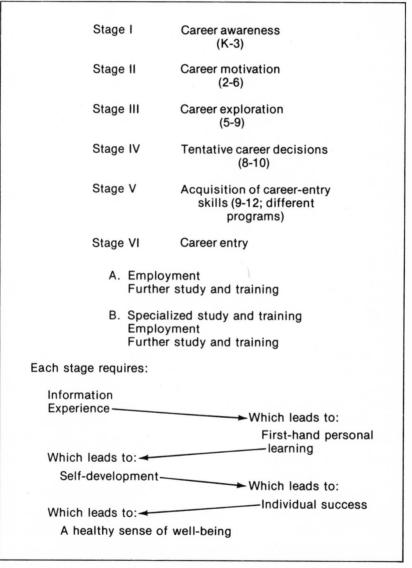

Figure 4.14. Career Education in Louisiana:
An Experience-Based, Sequential Plan

(4) A realistic understanding of the world of work and education which assists individuals in becoming contributing members of society

(5) The ability to enter employment in a selected occupational area or to go on for further education

Such a system, it was hoped, would serve to (1) increase career options of students, (2) assist students in making decisions regarding careers, and (3) prepare students to enter suitable employment or go on to the next level of education.

The conceptual model of comprehensive career education in Figure 4.15 shows the heavy emphasis placed upon guidance, even in the elementary grades. In addition, the participating school systems and the Center for Vocational and Technical Education in Ohio have listed eight elements to be infused into all courses at each grade level, with their anticipated outcomes:

Career Education Elements	*Element Outcome*
Career awareness — knowledge of the total spectrum	Career identity — role or roles within the world of work
Self-awareness — knowledge of the components that make up self	Self-identity — know oneself; consistent value system
Appreciations and attitudes — life roles; feeling toward self and others in respect to society and economics	Self- and social fulfillment — active (thus satisfying) work role
Decision-making skills — applying information to rational processes to reach decisions	Career decisions — career direction; has a plan for career development
Economic awareness — perception of processes in production, distribution, consumption	Economic understanding — solve personal and social problems in an economic environment
Skill awareness and beginning competencies — skills; ways in which humans extend their behavior	Employment skills — competence in performance of job-related tasks
Employable skills — social and communications skills appropriate to career placement	Career placement — employed in line with career development plan
Educational awareness — perception of relationships between education and life	Educational identity — ability to select educational avenues to develop career plans

From these eight elements, there have been developed 32 themes, about fifteen hundred goals, and three thousand be-

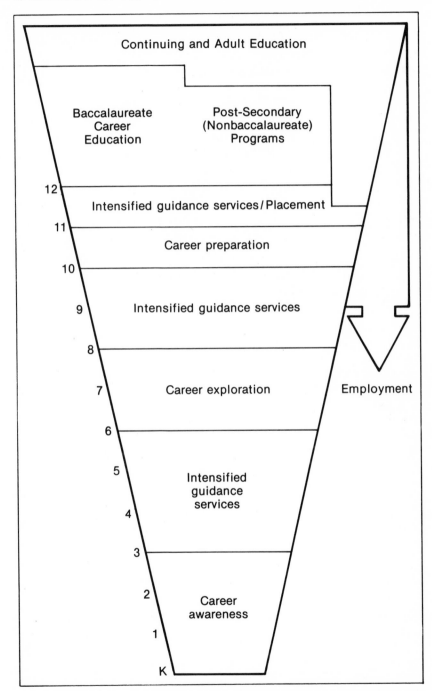

Figure 4.15. A Comprehensive Career Education System

havioral objectives. The initial products of this effort are to be made available to schools.

Model II: Employer-Based Career Education

The employer-based career education model seeks to serve secondary school students through an optional out-of-school program. A program format has been established which provides the necessary lifetime skills via arrangements with the business and industry community and the schools. Career skills development is being accomplished in real-life occupational settings by business and industry, with the schools being responsible for the related academic training. This model is intended as a provision for personalized education experience through existing curriculum and actual work through adult activities that are managed by employers. The model has four objectives:

(1) To provide an alternative educational program for students in an employer-based setting

(2) To unify the positive elements of academic, general, and vocational curriculums into a comprehensive career education program

(3) To increase the relevance of education as it applies to the world of work

(4) To broaden the base of community participation, particularly by involving public and private employers more directly and significantly in education

The employer-based model was considered a "top priority" by the National Institute of Education during fiscal year 1974. Contractual arrangements have been made to test it by consortia of public and private businesses and other organizations, including several of the regional educational laboratories.

Model III: Home- and Community-Based Career Education

The home- and community-based model is designed to provide career options to persons eighteen to 25 years of age, using the home as a center of learning. This program will assist adults

in identifying their aspirations and in matching their capabilities, experiences, and motivations to select and progress
through an appropriate educational program. These programs
will rely upon mass media found in the home, such as television
and radio, and those that can be brought into the home, such
as videotapes and cassettes. Career clinics within the community for appropriate career counseling are also to be
available.

The objective of this model is fivefold:

(1) To develop educational delivery systems for the home
and the community

(2) To provide new career education programs for adults

(3) To establish a guidance and career placement system to
assist individuals in occupational and related life roles

(4) To develop workers who have greater competencies

(5) To enhance the quality of the home as a learning center

Model IV: A Rural Residential Model

This model is being developed by the Mountain-Plains
Education and Economic Development Program, Incorporated, and is located at Glasgow, Montana, on the site of a
deactivated Air Force base. The model focuses on providing
rural disadvantaged families with the necessary employment
capabilities, on providing leverage for economic development
in the area, and on improving family living. Families are
selected from a six-state region — Idaho, Montana, Nebraska,
North Dakota, South Dakota, and Wyoming.

The program for this model is built round the needs of
each family, based upon information from interviews; personal
data; family interests, needs, and aptitudes; and available
resources. Families are exposed to a program which leads them
through occupational awareness, exploration, and preparation
in the areas of tourism, public services, and health. Additional
training is centered round family activities such as money
management, food planning and preparation, personal grooming, home planning and care, health education, and physical
fitness.

Career Education Components

In order for local education agencies to implement career education, they must be required to review their mission and restructure their curriculums. Top priority must be given to changing the attitudes of staff and providing adequate time for them to develop curriculums. A new role will evolve through cooperative efforts of the community and the schools, and career education will have to be moved into the mainstream of the educational process. To accomplish this task, Hoyt *et al.* (1974) have identified five necessary components: (1) the classroom teacher, (2) vocational skills training, (3) career development, (4) the home and family, and (5) the working community. The following discussion demonstrates how the five components should facilitate the integration of career education into the education system.

The Classroom Teacher

Career education asks that every classroom teacher in every course at every grade level emphasize the appropriate career implications of the particular subject being taught. With this career education emphasis, relevancy will be added to otherwise abstract academic subject matter, and the potential for more effective employment skills will be realized. It will be possible for all teachers to answer the question: Why do we teacher what we teach?

Hoyt and his associates have pointed out that career education is not intended to minimize the importance of the substantive content which teachers seek to help students learn, but instead is a way to help students learn more of the content. It may be appropriate to reorganize the educational content in such a manner that all students see the relationship between education and making a living.

Career education may ask some classroom teachers to modify, redirect, or reemphasize certain efforts. To the question — "What does career education expect the classroom teacher to do?" — the following seven points are significant:

(1) Career education expects teachers to embrace career education and adopt its basic assumptions and goals.

It asks teachers to search their own conscience, their professional convictions regarding the reasons why they have chosen to teach, the current conditions existing in their schools, the current needs of their students, and the rapidly changing needs of society that have resulted in the current career education emphasis.

(2) It asks classroom teachers to become aware of and knowledgeable about the career implications of the substantive content they seek to help students learn. This may call for extra time and effort on the part of the teacher, since few know about the "real" world of work, having spent their workday in the schoolroom.

(3) Classroom teachers must seek out and capitalize upon the wide variety of means available for emphasizing the career implications of the substantive content they seek to help students learn. Students will begin to learn through experiences that pertain to a career or careers. New teaching strategies will be needed to introduce the career implications to students in an interesting and meaningful approach.

(4) Career education asks the classroom teacher to emphasize these implications in ways that will bring dignity to all honest work and to all workers. Students will see themselves as prospective workers and will see work itself as a positive aspect of our society.

(5) Classroom teachers should emphasize career implications as a means of motivating students to learn more of the substantive content the teacher is attempting to teach. This approach should add to, not detract from, the opportunity for students to learn the subject matter. Students should be further motivated because of the relationship between what is being taught and its meaning to them as potential workers.

(6) Career education asks the teacher to seek out and capitalize upon cooperative activities involving the efforts of several teachers, or the entire teaching staff of the school, in order to emphasize career implications to students. Results of these efforts will be a curriculum

which is articulated from grade to grade, using the strengths of the teaching staff.

(7) Finally, the classroom teacher needs to work cooperatively with those charged with responsibility for the other career education components. Teachers must seek ways of working cooperatively with other teachers, the business-industry-labor community, counselors, other supporting school staff, and parents. By bringing together these components, teachers will find that learning will become meaningful to all students.

This curriculum component does not attempt to add more content; rather, it is intended to infuse career implications and career information into the existing curriculum. In order to achieve this infusion, in-service education will be needed to acquaint teachers with the concepts of career education. Appropriate time should be available beyond the school year for teachers to make necessary adjustments in their curriculum, thus capitalizing upon community and reference resources. Also, modifications will have to be made in teacher education programs if future teachers are to be prepared to cope with career education.

Vocational Skills Training

This component of career education is perceived as being infused into the present curriculum by all classroom teachers. Vocational skills training is intended to emphasize the concept that whenever one is acquiring skills related to a proposed area of occupational choice, he or she is engaged in vocational skills training.

At the elementary level, the student is helped to become aware of the occupations in the community. The prime purpose at this level is to help students become aware of the occupational world, to help them become familiar with the values of a work-oriented society, and to incorporate such values into their personal value structures. Students should be motivated by parents and by using various community resources in the effort.

Vocational skills training at the junior high school level has as its prime purpose teaching students the basic vocational skills which have applicability to broad families of occupations. These experiences will help students decide, from among such broad families, those that they might wish to pursue during the senior high school years. Students should be permitted to explore several of the fifteen clusters.

Vocational education is a part of this component. The traditional vocational education programs found at the secondary school level must be expanded to provide entry-level skills development in all fifteen clusters. In addition to manipulative skills, vocational skills should include knowledge, communicative skills, work attitudes, computational skills, and human relations and other learnings. Upon completion of the secondary level, students should possess the skills necessary to pursue their career choice through avenues of employment, community technical colleges, or four-year colleges or universities.

Career Development

This component of career development is of importance because it involves the guiding and shaping of one's life. The term "career development" refers to the total constellations of events, circumstances, and experiences of the individuals as they make decisions about themselves as prospective and actual members of the work force. In this situation, guidance and counseling will take on a new emphasis. Informal counseling may be provided by all classroom teachers, with the formal aspects being supplied by guidance personnel.

Career development must be fully understood before it can be carried out. Hoyt *et al.* (1974) explained the basic nature of this component in the following:

(1) Career development is a lifelong process which begins early in the preschool years and continues for most individuals through retirement.

(2) Personal choices are taking place on a continuing basis throughout the life of the individual.

(3) Occupational choices are expressed in many forms and with many degrees of firmness and insight at various times in the life of the individual.

(4) Choices are made on the basis of what individuals would enjoy doing, on the basis of what appears possible for them to do, given their personal and societal limitation and strengths, and on the basis of what is important for each individual.

(5) The prime goal of career development lies in its process, not its end result. The important thing is that the individual chooses, not *what* the individual chooses.

(6) The wisdom of career choice lies in the extent to which and the basis on which it is a reasoned choice, not in the degree to which it seems reasonable to others.

Through career development, students will be making appropriate career plans. Programs of study will be arranged to fulfill the student's career plan. The end result will be students better prepared upon high school graduation to pursue their career plan through employment, community or technical colleges, or four-year college and meet the demands placed upon them by society.

The Home and Family

The home and family can be of considerable help in furthering educational objectives. It can also help schools achieve the goals of career education. The capacity of parents to influence the child's attitude, planning, and coping behavior should be recognized and used as an integral part of the educational process.

Parents can share their occupational roles with students through classroom and on-the-job activities. Few students have a good idea of the specific nature of their parents' occupations. Classroom teachers and counselors should use parents as resources in the curriculum. Schools could, with the proper approval of employers, have the opportunity of using the occupational facilities of parents for student learning activities.

Through the combined efforts of the school and parents, a new dimension will be added to the classroom, one that will have the endorsement and reinforcement of the educational objectives of the home and family.

Contributions of the Working Community

The classroom will be extended beyond the four walls of the schoolbuilding through this component of career education. Business and labor must become an integral part of the career education program. Provisions should permit the students to be active through work observation, work experience, work study, and cooperative education programs. Also, community personnel might be members of a career education advisory committee, which would provide input into the education agency. The community might provide resource personnel and materials to assist classroom teachers in giving career implications to their existing curriculums. Finally, exchange programs between schools and the community should be arranged to provide the classroom teacher experiences which will help relate subject content to the working world. Through cooperative efforts, students will become prepared employees with the skills to make them productive, successful, and satisfied members of our working society.

Summary

Career education is a comprehensive effort to integrate concepts into the existing curriculum of our education system. Programs will be restructured round the theme of career development, including opportunities and requirements in the world of work. A blending of vocational, academic, and counseling activities needs to be achieved to provide relevancy for students to help them see the relationship to future career goals. Elementary grades will be organized round the wide range of occupations in our economy and the associated societal roles. In the junior high school, students will prepare for their chosen career cluster with options available to them upon graduation in the areas of employment, community technical colleges, or four-year colleges or universities. These efforts can be reached only through involvement of every classroom teacher's providing vocational skills training. Assistance is needed from guidance personnel in the area of career development for each student, along with cooperative efforts of the whole community.

Finally, parent involvement is essential because of parents' influence on attitudes and actions of students.

The models, elements, and characteristics presented in this chapter may serve to provide additional guidelines and insights for everyone concerned about identifying or developing ways to achieve a more meaningful and more responsive education system.

Selected References

Alabama State Department of Education. *Career Education in Alabama: The Art of the State.* Montgomery: Alabama State Department of Education. 1974.

Bottoms, Gene. *Career Development Education: Kindergarten through Post-Secondary and Adult Levels.* Atlanta: Georgia Department of Education. 1973.

Budke, Wesley; *et al. Career Education Practices.* Columbus: Ohio State University, Center for Vocational and Technical Education. 1972.

Edington, Everett; and Conley, Howard K. *Career Education Handbook for Rural School Administrators.* Las Cruces: New Mexico State University, ERIC Clearinghouse on Rural Education and Small Schools. 1973.

Goldhammer, Keith; and Taylor, Robert E. *Career Education: Promise and Perspective.* Columbus, Ohio: Charles E. Merrill Books, Inc. 1972.

Hoyt, Kenneth B.; *et al. Career Education and the Elementary School Teacher.* Salt Lake City: Olympus Publishing Company. 1973.

_____; *et al. Career Education: What It Is and How to Do It.* Second edition. Salt Lake City: Olympus Publishing Company. 1974.

Kansas State Department of Education. *The Kansas Guide for Career Education.* Topeka: Kansas State Department of Education. 1973.

Keller, Louise J. *Career Education In-Service Training Guide.* General Learning Corporation. 1972.

Kunzman, Leonard. *Career Education in Oregon: A Statement on Improvement of Vocational Instruction in Oregon Schools.* Salem: Oregon Board of Education. 1970.

_____. *Guide: Career Education Development in Oregon.* Salem: Oregon Board of Education.

McClure, Larry; and Buan, Carolyn. Editors. *Essays on Career Education.* Portland, Oregon: Northwest Regional Educational Laboratory. 1973.

McMinn, J. H. *Career Education in Mississippi.* Jackson: Mississippi State Department of Education. 1973.

Michot, Louis. *State Plan for Career Education.* Baton Rouge: Louisiana State Department of Education. 1973.

Miller, A. J. "A Synthesis of Research in Progress on the National Career Education Models." Paper presented at the Fifth Annual National Leadership Development Seminar for State Directors of Vocational Education. Columbus, Ohio, September 19 to 22, 1972.

Nevada State Department of Education. *Career Development in Nevada.* Carson City: Nevada State Department of Education. 1973.

Ohio Department of Education. *Career Motivation: Curriculum Guide for Grades K-6.* Columbus: Ohio Department of Education. 1972.

Ohio State University. *Developmental Program Goals for the Comprehensive Career Education Model.* Columbus: Ohio State University, Center for Vocational and Technical Education. 1972.

Porter, John W. "Career Education." *Michigan School Board Journal* (October 1973).

Rasmussen, Marvin; and Carpenter, Leonard. *A Program of Career Education in the Portland Public Schools.* Portland, Oregon: Portland Public Schools. 1971.

Searcy, Ellen. *Work Experience as Preparation for Adulthood.* Washington, D.C.: George Washington University, Social Research Group. 1973.

Simpson, Elizabeth J. "The Home as a Career Education Center." *Exceptional Children* (May 1973).

U.S. Department of Health, Education, and Welfare. *Career Education: A Model for Implementation.* Washington, D.C.: U.S. Department of Health, Education, and Welfare, Office of Education, Bureau of Adult, Vocational, and Technical Education. 1971.

Wisconsin Department of Public Instruction. *K–12 Guide for Integrating Career Development into Local Curriculum.* Madison: Wisconsin Department of Public Instruction. 1971.

5

Career Education and the State Education Agency

David L. Jesser
E. Niel Carey*

The rationale for career education, as it has been presented in this book and elsewhere, includes an impressive list of human needs and societal problems which may to a considerable degree be met or solved by directing proper attention to the career development of individuals. The human needs include: the need to know about one's own attributes and interests — which have both potential and implications for career satisfaction; the need to know in a meaningful way about the broad range of available life career options; and the need to be able to make and then implement rational decisions, including those related to life career options and choices.

While many educators and educational institutions are making serious efforts to meet the *human* needs, there still remain in nearly every community highly visible signs which are indicative of the extent or degree to which many of the human needs remain unmet. Throughout society, there are students who proceed mechanically through the several levels of the education system with no real sense of direction, purpose, or goals. Many such students, upon exiting from the educational arena and entering the broader societal structure, find themselves incapable of dealing or coping with the com-

*Specialist in Vocational Guidance and Chairman, Career Education Task Force, Maryland State Department of Education.

133

plexities of the "real world." And society is then assigned the responsibility of caring for their needs.

In addition, in nearly every community, the unemployment rate of youth continues inordinately high — even though there are many job openings not being filled. There are of course some valid but perhaps indefensible reasons for this situation, but most would seem to revolve round two themes that are products of the society: job stereotyping and unrealistic expectations. Both of these result in frustration and in some instances rather traumatic experiences within the youth group. But again, it is society which ultimately must assume the responsibility of caring for needs of individuals who are unable to "cope."

And indeed of equal seriousness in modern society is the problem faced by the large numbers of adults who, after having worked for many years, suddenly find their acquired and accumulated skills to be outmoted or obsolete, and hence they are no longer employable. Many aerospace engineers in Seattle and Cape Canaveral found themselves in this category when the supersonic transport program was discontinued and when the Apollo program was completed. Many employees in other industries are facing similar situations because of the continuing refinement and installation of automation. Again, if and when such people became employable, society has to assume the responsibility of helping them.

These and other related factors, plus the public's consistent and persistent expectation that the schools — the education system — should prepare those who are involved for economic self-sufficiency, provide strong incentives for educational leadership to designate career education as a major priority in American education. The economic motivation, obviously, is and should be a strong base for career education efforts in the public schools. However, care must be taken to keep economic motivation from being the only base.

As suggested earlier, there are *human* needs, and some of these transcend economic needs. Educational leadership, as it moves toward assigning high-priority status to career education, must also keep in mind the other (in addition to economic) returns that can accrue to society if and when the concept that has been presented is transformed into a reality. In this regard, a major goal, both practical and realistic, for education should relate to the development of human excellence, of which intellectual and occupational development constitute only parts — essential as they may be — of an overarching whole. Charles Reich (1970, pp. 5–6) highlighted this thought in *The Greening of America* when he observed that:

> ...today's emerging consciousness seeks a new knowledge of what it means to be human, in order that the machine, having been built, may now be turned to human ends; in order that man once more can become a creative force, renewing and creating his own life and thus giving life back to his society.

Career education, as it has been conceived, propounded, perceived, and developed, holds great promise for meeting economic needs of individuals, human and humane needs of people, and perhaps more importantly, needs of society. But if the ideal of a renewed education system — one that is capable of helping to meet those needs and at the same time is commensurate with the aptitudes, needs, and interests of those it is designed to serve — is to be reached, it is imperative that educational leadership act promptly. Every educator who is charged with the responsibility for helping individuals — young and old alike — to learn must perceive the total educational process as preparation for a total life pattern. Each must also be willing and able to perceive that an individual's life pattern will in all probability revolve round one's career.

The preceding in no way rejects or negates other conceptualizations relating to the aims of education. There are, and should be, valid aims concerning personal enlightenment, social and physical development, and exploration of the realms of knowledge. These are all viable and desirable aims and lend support to the recognition that education must exist in many different forms; that no one form will be exactly right for everyone. But while there will be differing forms of education in order that the varying needs of individuals may better be served, recognition of the relationship between education and one's life career pattern should provide the basic framework into which all education might fit.

In this context, it would seem clear that career education, as it has been explained here and elsewhere, could provide for or accommodate a large portion of the framework for education. Career education encompasses the full range of educational endeavor — from preschool through the adult years. And it calls for education systems to be diverse in their organization so that they are able to provide for the wide range of options and opportunities that will be required.

Career education holds great promise. But while advocating its acceptance, educational leaders must avoid the temptation (as has been the case with many other educational innovations) to view it as a cure-all or panacea that will cause all of the problems facing education to disappear. As William Pierce, Deputy Commissioner for Occupational and Adult Education (USOE), has observed:

> Career education is nevertheless no magic potion. It is not going to open doors for college students receiving their A.B. degrees this June or for youngsters getting their high school diplomas. Given the increasing interest in the concept, however, and in the spirit and point of view that lie behind it, we can hope that the day is not too distant when no student will leave the classroom with the feeling that he has simply been cast adrift. Perhaps at that time a nascent English teacher will not have to wonder, as our baby-sitter did, why she had been required to learn where Russia's principal minerals are to be found.

The State Education Agency

Toward the ends that have been described, and with the help of the educational leadership represented in the various state and extra-state (territorial) education agencies, considerable progress has been made in the entire career education thrust throughout the nation. The progress has been especially marked during the past five years.

For purposes of illustrating the kind of progress that has taken place, one should consider the fact that in 1968 there existed only one state education agency which had recognized the importance of career education by designating a staff member to be responsible for its development in the state. By 1973, well over half of the state education agencies had created such positions, and in 1974, nearly every such agency was able to name a professional staff member as being responsible for career education.

By way of further illustrating the progress that has been made, one should consider the fact that in 1973 over half of the state education agencies had developed both position statements and state plans relating to career education; this, from a virtual zero point in 1968. And similarly by 1973, roughly a third of the state education agencies had identifiable budgets to be used for the support of career education. And by 1973, well over half of the state education agencies had established career education as a major educational priority.

But while much has already been accomplished in the area of career education, a great deal more remains to be accomplished before learners — at whatever educational level, and irrespective of sex, race, ethnic origin, or socioeconomic or cultural status — will have anything approaching equal access to educational programs designed to meet career development needs.

The state education agency, having as it does the primary responsibility for the educational program of the state, is in an advantageous position to plan for, initiate, and facilitate the implementation of career education. It is in reality the only education agency capable of influencing, and changing where necessary, educational programs provided for total state populations.

The preceding should in no way imply that needed educational changes — such as career education — can *only* be initiated by the state education agency. To infer that this is the case would be tragic; to believe that such is the case would be unpropitious. If, as Hoyt *et al.* (1974) suggest, career education represents a "response to a call for educational reform," the call, together with a suggested reform — i.e., career education — can be voiced from virtually any segment of society, as is suggested in Figure 5.1.

In some states, the initial call for career education may have been made by the legislature; in others, it might have been voiced by business, labor, or community organizations; and in others, it may have been called for by the governor. But while the initial impetus may be generated or supplied by

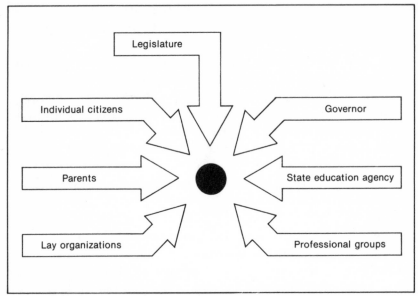

Figure 5.1. Segments of Society That Could Initiate
Changes in the Education System

a variety of sources, and if the utlimate goal is to involve *every* learner, it is the state education agency that must assume and assert its leadership role.

Strategies for State Education Agencies

As state and extra-state education agencies have begun to implement or further strengthen the concept of career education in the educational programs, various strategies have been employed.

Board Resolution and Legislative Directive

In some states, and especially those in which progress (in terms of career education) has been somewhat marked, a basic and initial strategy involved securing support, by means of adoption of a resolution or approval of a position statement, by the state board of education. In Maryland, as one example, the state board of education adopted a resolution relating to career education in 1971. A copy of the Maryland resolution is reproduced in Figure 5.2. In others, the initial strategy consisted of securing legislative approval (and, it was hoped, legis-

---

**Resolution
Maryland State Board of Education
October 27, 1971**

Resolution No. 1971-56   Re: **Career Education**

WHEREAS, the central purposes of education — to prepare youth to accept the reality of constructive pathways to adulthood, to help them to engage these pathways successfully, and to assist them in finding personal relevance in the life options to them — are not being effectively accomplished for large numbers of youth in the school system of our State, and

WHEREAS, one of the goals toward which our education system must direct itself is the provision for every student to acquire the skills which will allow him to make a livelihood for himself and for his future family, no matter at what level of education system he leaves, and

WHEREAS, such skills are not confined to the manipulative skills but are all those by which one can use his capabilities in activities which contribute both to individual fulfillment and society's maintenance and progress, and

WHEREAS, to make public education in Maryland became more relevant to today's needs and the needs of the future, it becomes increasingly evident that public education should be focused round the theme of career education, and

WHEREAS, the Maryland State Department of Education has been singularly honored by being selected as the agency to bring this matter to the attention of key educators and decision makers across the nation, now therefore

BE IT RESOLVED, that the State Board affirms its support of the concept of career education and directs the Department to develop a comprehensive plan to serve all youth and adults involving career orientation, exploration, preparation for job entry or further education, including intensive guidance and counseling services.

Figure 5.2. Resolution Adopted by the Maryland
State Board of Education

lative appropriations) in support of the concept. Support of this nature is illustrated by a resolution introduced recently in the Kansas State Legislature as shown in Figure 5.3. It should be noted that none of the strategies, i.e., state, local, or legislative, would in all likelihood be successfully developed without the leadership of the state education agency.

Task Force Approach

Other strategies developed have related to acquainting departmental personnel with and involving them in the concept that career education *does* offer viable and desirable alternatives to the existing educational program; that career education is not intended to supplant or replace the existing program, but instead is meant to strengthen and bolster it. In state education agencies where this strategy has been employed, interdisciplinary task forces have been created to study, define, and develop long-range plans for career education. The Maryland State Department of Education, for example, created such a task force which in turn developed a comprehensive five-year plan for career education in the state. The Kansas State Department of Education created a task force on career education that has worked closely with a broad-based state task force and has developed a three-year plan for the department.

Several other states, including California and Utah, have also used the task force approach and have been able to deal with related problems. This strategy — creation and use of a broad-based or interdisciplinary task force — is usually an effective means of securing sound advice and guidelines, as well as broad-based support.

Assessment of Need, Dissemination, and Involvement

In determining or assessing the need for career education, numerous state education agencies have made widespread use of advisory groups, citizens' committees, governor's conferences, and the like. This strategy obviously holds the same type of potential as the task force approach. It is, however, much broader and more representative in scope. Through the use of citizen groups, either at the state or local level, it is

Senate Concurrent Resolution No. 82
By Senator Harder
1-11

A CONCURRENT RESOLUTION requesting the state board of education to encourage, support and promote career education programs in Kansas school districts.

WHEREAS, More than one-half of all youths in the United States who end their schooling each year have no salable skill or training with which to earn a living, and

WHEREAS, Public school programs historically have been primarily college preparatory with only secondary and limited emphasis placed on vocational education and such programs have not responded to the needs of a great number of the youths who pass through the school system, and

WHEREAS, Teacher training institutions generally have not placed significant emphasis on a career awareness component in teacher preparation programs, and

WHEREAS, Public school programs, publicly supported vocational schools and state colleges and universities have not been able to keep pace in their educational programs with changing job requirements and labor market demands: Now, therefore,

Be it resolved by the Senate of the State of Kansas, the House of Representatives concurring therein: That, in recognition by the Legislature of the State of Kansas of the urgent need for incorporation into the public school system of the concepts of career education, including career awareness and career preparation and exploration, the state board of education is herewith requested to provide further leadership in the field of career education so that state goals and objectives can be implemented in the school districts of Kansas at the earliest practicable time. In recognition of the fact that the state board of education already has articulated statewide goals for career education and has cooperated in the operation of several individual career education projects, including in-service training sessions, the state board of education is further requested to prepare and submit to the 1974 Legislature a proposed action program containing a detailed funding proposal designed as expeditiously as possible to make career education opportunities available to all students of Kansas school districts; encourage post-secondary institutions to incorporate into their teacher training programs effective career education preparation opportunities; prepare guidelines to assist school districts in planning and organizing career education programs; provide in-service and other programs as may be necessary to reorient teachers serving in the field; prepare, publish and otherwise disseminate materials for continuing education of school personnel; evaluate the effectiveness of school district career education programs; and provide such further state-level direction and leadership as will bring the full benefits of career education to the youth of this state.

Be it further resolved: That the secretary of state is hereby directed to transmit a copy of this resolution to the chairman of the state board of regents, the chairman of the state board of education and to the commissioner of education for duplication and transmittal to every school board member within the state of Kansas.

Figure 5.3. Resolution Introduced by the
Kansas State Legislature

possible for a state education agency to enlist the help and support of many people in:

(1) Assessing the career needs of individuals for whom the education system is responsible, including those sub-populations having special career needs

(2) Developing and articulating goals of and for the education system which are more likely to accommodate the identified career needs of the population(s)

(3) Determining the degree to which the education system is or is not achieving the goals which have been identified

When this strategy is used in order to determine or assess the need for career education, there will obviously be a built-in mechanism for real involvement and for dissemination of information about career education as well. Through well-planned and organized question and answer sessions, those responsible for career education will have an opportunity to assist the general public in understanding the educational potential that career education holds for meeting the needs of the learners as well as the goals of education.

In Texas, for example, the state education agency, with the help of hundreds of citizens from round the state, was able to develop a series of learner outcomes. These reflected what the citizens expected the products of the education system to "look like" upon exit. The information gained was compiled and published in a monograph titled *Basic Learner Outcomes for Career Education* (1973), and in this form has been valuable in giving the agency, together with the public school systems, a sense of need and direction. In this effort, the elements of needs assessment, dissemination, and involvement were clearly visible.

A strategy aimed more at involvement and dissemination has recently been developed and used in both Minnesota and Texas. In these states, television commercial-type "spots" have been prepared and shown on the television stations through-out the state. In each instance, the spot deals with some aspect of the concept of career education and then invites the viewer to contact the state education agency (or the regional service center) for further information. In the case of Minnesota, a grant for the purpose of preparing the "commercials" was obtained from one of the large corporations in that state. As a result of efforts such as these, it has been possible to disseminate information about and involve citizens in career education in a contemporary mode.

The strategy discussed here has to this point been directed primarily toward lay citizens. This is not to suggest that it be used only with lay people. Professional educators – classroom teachers, building principals, district administrators, college professors, and state education agency personnel – can and should be involved in much the same manner. The Chamber of Commerce of the United States, in a recent publication titled *Blueprint for the Possible*, provides some clues as to how groups of professional educators might help to determine what needs might exist, and at the same time might themselves become more aware of the needs. For example, a simple questionnaire might be developed and administered to ascertain if, or to what degree:

(1) The school system has worked with employer groups to determine entry-level requirements for specific jobs and occupations for graduates

(2) The school system provides parents with information on each student's aptitude as a basis for career guidance

(3) The school system has established business, industry, and community groups on career education

(4) The school system provides a job placement service and works with public employment service centers for its prospective graduates and students who leave before completion of formal schooling

(5) Business and industry have been involved in planning career education programs with the school system

(6) The school system has explored the feasibility of establishing "classrooms" outside of the school – in plants, offices, and the various social and governmental agencies

(7) The school system makes use of volunteers from industry and from government and social agencies as visiting or adjunct instructors

Obviously, the statements used here (and adapted from the U.S. Chamber of Commerce publication) are leading ones. They can, however, serve as a model for obtaining information relating to need, for providing school systems with clues as to how they might proceed, or for creating among educators an awareness of a need that perhaps had not been previously recognized. Any of the three seems to be of considerable value in a strategy aimed at assessment of need, dissemination, and meaningful involvement.

In-Service Programs for Teachers

This strategy, while closely related to the one just discussed, is of primary importance because in the final analysis it is the classroom teacher who will or will not make career education a reality for every learner. Classroom teachers therefore must be helped to understand what career education is and what it is not, what is involved in its process, who is responsible for it, what materials are available to help learners achieve its goals, and where they can find resources that will facilitate accomplishment of goals and attainment of purposes.

In nearly every state where significant progress in career education efforts has been made, the state education agency has made good use of this strategy. In Ohio, for example, there is an ongoing in-service program for those who have system-wide responsibilities and those who have building responsibilities. Industry, business, and government agencies are brought into play, and every attempt is made to acquaint the educators with possible answers to the problems discussed above.

With support and encouragement from state education agency personnel, Ohio educators having responsibility for local in-service programs have demonstrated how resourceful and creative they can be. In one school system, the career education coordinator discovered (to his amazement and dismay) that few if any of the elementary teachers — who were to have the responsibility of acquainting the youngsters with the world of work — had had any work experience other than teaching. As a result, and with the cooperation of a nearby university and the business and industry community, some sixteen teachers each spent about three weeks learning firsthand about

manufacturing, banking, sales, and so forth (de Gulio and Zockel, 1973).

Other state education agencies, such as in Texas and Oregon, have developed and used in-service programs with the help of regional educational units within the state. In Oregon, for example, each of the regional units has a person responsible for career education in the area served by the regional unit. These educators meet regularly with state agency personnel to learn about new developments (in curriculum, for example), and return to their own regions to work directly with the teachers in the local schools and school systems. Similar patterns are followed in Texas. This approach to in-service programs obviously greatly expands the capabilities of state education agency personnel.

Still other state education agencies either sponsor directly— or facilitate the sponsorship of — in-service programs in career education for teachers and entire faculties as the occasion warrants. In any event and in every instance, the strategy involving such programs should be well conceived and should represent the best effort possible to acquaint educators with the points enumerated earlier.

Career education for most teachers represents a change. And people, including teachers, are likely to accept and support a change to the extent that they understand the need for it. In this context, an in-service strategy can be crucial.

Sources of Funding

It is well to consider strategies that will provide for the implementation or expansion of career education programs in a state. The need for such strategies should be obvious. But at the same time, it should be equally obvious that most of the strategies that might or should be used reflect a need for funds for their support. In some cases, the funds needed might be perceived as "in addition to" existing funds. In other instances, the needed funds may be derived through a reallocation of certain funds that are already available.

As career education efforts were initiated by many state education agencies, funds were made available for this purpose from vocational education monies. To a large extent, this practice has continued in quite a few states. But as the concept of

career education has gained a broader acceptance, state legislatures have begun to appropriate funds specifically for career education purposes. In Louisiana, for example, the legislature appropriated some $8 million in order that career education might be developed and implemented statewide, with provision for similar appropriations over a period of several years. The Arizona Legislature, in similar fashion, has made multimillion dollar appropriations to support the career education efforts in that state. In Ohio, state funds have been appropriated for career education on a per-pupil basis. In still other states, specific funds have been made available for planning efforts in career education. And in many state education agencies, budgets for career education efforts have been created by redirecting some of the existing funds.

The funding strategy for career education efforts in a state is vital to the success of those efforts. In developing such a strategy, state education agency personnel should make every effort to clearly identify the funds that will be needed, how they will be used, and what results might be expected as a result of the expenditure of the funds. They should then seek out the most logical source or combination of sources and proceed in their attempts to secure the needed monies.

Evaluation and Accountability

The essentiality of both evaluation and accountability was discussed in chapter 3, but it was discussed primarily in the context of curriculum development. A state education agency, responsible as it is for ensuring the best possible educational opportunities for the learners, must develop and use procedures that will enable it to know that this is happening. This is true of the total educational program. It is especially true of career education — a relatively new concept in education for which funds are being sought.

To date, few state education agencies have been able to mount full-scale evaluative efforts in the area of career education. At the moment, this is understandable, because of the recency of the implementation of career education. But as efforts in career education become more institutionalized and widespread, there will undoubtedly be many concerned citizens, legislators, and educators who will want to know if the

dollars invested in career education are really paying off. Forward-looking state education agency personnel will anticipate this and will have developed a strategy that will enable them to have ready — and defensible — answers.

Teacher Preparation Programs

It is true that many state education agencies do not have direct responsibility for institutions of higher learning, including those which offer teacher preparation programs. It is equally true, however, that they are responsible for the institutions which use the products of those teacher training programs. It would seem plausible, then, for the state education agency to be able to influence, to some degree, the content of teacher preparation programs.

In several states, including Colorado, Ohio, and Nevada, there have been established cooperative working relationships, and the state education agencies have been able to bring about a degree of awareness of the need for teachers who, upon entry into the field, will understand the concept of career education.

In at least two states, however, the efforts of the state education agency have gone far beyond the more or less informal arrangements that exist in most states. In Michigan and Washington, cooperative programs and consortia of certain institutions of higher learning have been developed under the leadership of the state education agency.

Arrangements such as those which have been created in these states hold considerable promise for the restructuring of teacher education programs that is needed if teachers are to be "career education oriented" before they accept their first teaching position. Again, forward-looking state education agency personnel will develop strategies designed to bring about such arrangements. The information about the Michigan effort (shown in Figure 5.4) will be of interest to such personnel.

Implications for State Education Agencies

Throughout this book there have been presented discussions relating to concepts, purposes, and models of career education. Earlier in this chapter several strategies that might be

Fact Sheet

What Is It?

The consortium is a cooperative organization formed by faculty representatives from eight of Michigan's largest teacher education institutions and a liaison from the Michigan Department of Education. The purpose of the consortium is to coordinate and plan personnel development efforts relevant to the implementation of the Michigan Career Education Model.

How Was It Formed?

The consortium grew out of a series of meetings held late in 1972 between Michigan's Superintendent of Public Instruction, Dr. John Porter, and the Deans of eight of Michigan's largest teacher education institutions.

What Is the Consortium's Goal?

The goal of the Career Education Teacher Education Consortium is to assist Michigan educators in increasing their capabilities to more adequately provide learning experiences to the children, youth, and adults in this State consistent with the goal of career education.

Who Are the Consortium Members?

Central Michigan University
Mt. Pleasant, Michigan

Eastern Michigan University
Ypsilanti, Michigan

Ferris State College
Big Rapids, Michigan

Michigan State University
East Lansing, Michigan

Northern Michigan University
Marquette, Michigan

University of Michigan
Ann Arbor, Michigan

Wayne State University
Detroit, Michigan

Western Michigan University
Kalamazoo, Michigan

Figure 5.4. Michigan's Career Education Teacher
Education Consortium

What Are the Consortium's Specific Objectives?

1. To provide Michigan's local education agencies with appropriate in-service assistance relative to their implementation of career education
2. To modify the pre-service programs of Michigan's educational personnel so as to better prepare these individuals so that they can work with Michigan's career education programs
3. To help local school districts in the design and implementation of career education programs
4. To inform university faculties about the concept and programs of Michigan's Career Education Model

How Are the Consortium Members Organized?

Each institution has a consortium representative appointed by the Dean of Education. Each institution has a career education cadre of 14 to 30 faculty members (across all fields of education and from fields outside professional education). These cadres work as a team to design personnel development materials, provide in-service help to local education agencies, and recommend changes in the pre-service teacher preparation program. The cadres also work with local districts under contract to the Michigan Department of Education to field develop and test various components of the Michigan Career Education Model. Finally, the cadres provide a variety of career education orientation activities for their fellow university faculty colleges.

What Has the Consortium Done to Date?

Besides the many accomplishments of the individual cadre, the consortium itself is currently engaged in designing packaged in-service material related to the awareness and understanding of career education. During the coming fiscal year, the consortium will participate in the development of similar packaged in-service material for infusion of career education, the use of performance-based instruction in career education, and the planning of career education programs. Each member will be training personnel to use these in-service materials and will provide many new services to local districts throughout 1974-75.

Where Can You Get Additional Information?

Contact the Michigan Department of Education liaison person.

Figure 5.4 (continued)

used by state education agencies to initiate, implement, or expand career education were also presented and discussed. All of these, obviously, have serious implications for state education agencies; most of the implications relating to these will not be discussed here. But there are, it would seem, several broader issues — implications — which should be brought out. These include those relating to implementation or expansion of career education on a truly statewide basis; those relating to funding sources or patterns for career education efforts; and those relating to the examination, evaluation, and improvement of career education efforts and programs throughout the state.

Implementation

According to Rasmussen and Carpenter (1971), in a recent descriptive account of career education in the Portland, Oregon, public schools, the implementation of career education programs, when contrasted with acceptance, is indeed a "different" matter. As they have perceptively observed:

> Even though there is widespread acceptance of career education as a function of the schools, it has largely remained isolated from the mainstream of the elementary and secondary curriculum. Too often it is still regarded as a last resort to keep youth from leaving school before graduation. *Obviously, career education has not taken its proper place among the programs of the schools* (emphasis added).

The concern raised by Rasmussen and Carpenter relates directly to a local school system. It is, however, quite valid in terms of career education efforts in many states. In fact, at a recent conference for state directors and coordinators of career education, the matter of implementation (and expansion of effort) was the most frequently mentioned concern.

It would seem, then, that state education agencies will need to examine the matter of implementation of career education from at least two points of view: (1) what steps might be taken to facilitate implementation at the state or agency level and (2) what steps might be taken, by the state education agency, to facilitate implementation at the local level.

An important and key element in both considerations relates to the notion of "facilitating," and obviously there are many ways of doing this — planning, funding, being involved, and the like. These should not be overlooked. But basic to all, on the part of the state education agency, would seem to revolve round patterns of organization that can be established within the agency itself and between it and other state agencies.

At the State Level

Within the Utah state education agency, for example, there was developed an organizational structure that was designed to define and delineate the roles and functions of all the divisions within the agency as they relate to career education. The structure (as seen in Figure 5.5) also provided for the establishment of a "career education planning staff," made up of the heads of several of the departmental divisions and regular career education personnel, and for a policy or governing board made up of the deputy superintendents.

Through the pattern of involvement and direct participation that is illustrated, it is possible to see how career education can be perceived as a departmental activity. When it is so perceived and is planned by a widely representative group of agency personnel, the process and probability of implementation on a statewide basis would seem to be greatly enhanced.

In terms of facilitating implementation of career education, a state education agency may also want to consider the possibility of establishing formal linkages with other state agencies or institutions having an interest in and a concern about career education. In Colorado, as one example of this approach, and as a result of a cooperatively developed state plan for career education, an organizational structure involving the cooperating agencies was created. In the Colorado approach (illustrated in Figure 5.6) relationships and basic responsibilities as they relate to the executive office, the department of education, the Commission on Higher Education, and the Board for Community Colleges and Occupational Education are defined.

Obviously, there are differing needs in the several states; thus the Colorado chart is not intended as a model. It is, how-

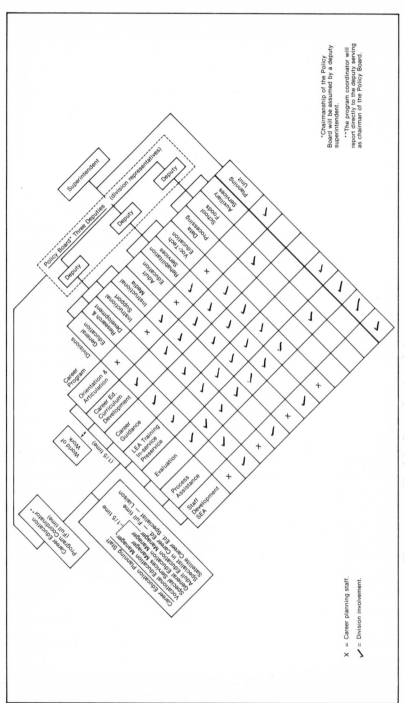

Figure 5.5. Utah's Organizational Structure for Career Education

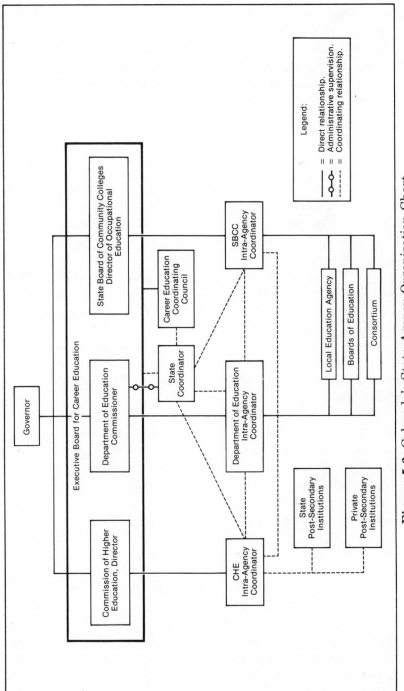

Figure 5.6. Colorado's State Agency Organization Chart

ever, intended to suggest the ways in which state education agencies might establish desirable linkages. Again, in establishing such linkages, a broad type of support can be achieved, and because the "performers" are also directly involved in the process, the possibility of statewide implementation of career education would seem to be enhanced.

At the Local Level

While organizational structures can be (and have been) created at the state level to facilitate implementation of career education, attention must be directed to local education agencies. It is, after all, at the local level — in schoolbuildings and classrooms — that major changes such as career education are ultimately implemented and effected.

How and in what ways might the state education agency assist the local education agency in implementing career education? Several possible ways or strategies have already been discussed; all should be seriously considered and used under appropriate circumstances. There is, however, one area in which most state education agencies can greatly assist local education agencies in implementing career education — the area of planning.

Many local schools and school systems already have a capability for planning. At the same time, however, many do not. Regardless of the existence of such a capability, every local school system could use to good advantage guides, checklists, and similar documents that might be prepared and distributed by the state education agency.

Toward this end, the Utah Department of Public Instruction, in cooperation with Georgia, New Jersey, Oregon, and Wisconsin, has developed a brochure titled "A Guide for the Implementation of Career Education in a Local Education Agency" (1973). The guide — which, it is hoped, will be available for general distribution in the near future — defines and explains the various steps which should be taken as the local agency prepares to implement career education. (The major steps are portrayed in the schematic shown in Figure 5.7. They are broken down into component steps and explained in the guide.)

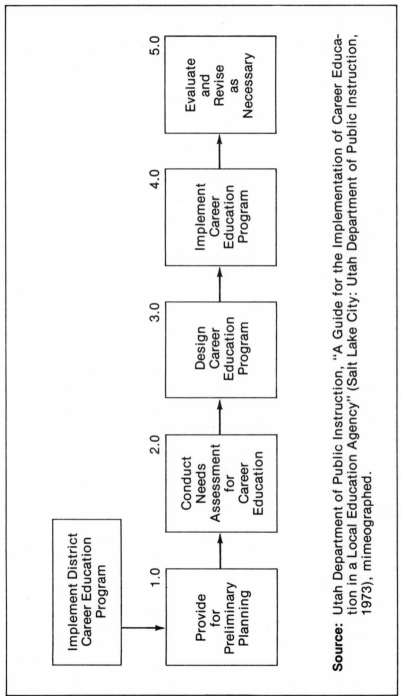

Figure 5.7. Major Steps in Implementing a District Career Education Program

Source: Utah Department of Public Instruction, "A Guide for the Implementation of Career Education in a Local Education Agency" (Salt Lake City: Utah Department of Public Instruction, 1973), mimeographed.

Legislative Support

In examining various ways in which the implementation process can be facilitated, one must not overlook the importance of enabling and supportive legislation. Through the leadership demonstrated by several state education agencies, several state legislatures have designed laws that are highly supportive of career education. In addition, the Senate's bill on education (S. 1539, being considered at this writing)* also contains provisions that are supportive of career education. Both kinds of efforts at the state and national levels are crucial to the overall success of career education, and educational leadership should continue to encourage them. It should be noted, however (as has apparently been thought in some instances), that implementation efforts do not end with legislation; they must still be made after the laws are passed.

Coordination of Effort

Attention should be given by state education agencies to the matter of coordination of effort with local agencies on the one hand and with national agencies on the other. In addition, as was demonstrated at the National Career Education Conference for State Directors and Coordinators in Dallas, Texas, on April 29 through May 1, 1974, there is also a need for coordination of effort, to the utmost degree possible, among the state education agencies as they continue to develop and implement programs of career education.

Funding

There may be those who would suggest that adequate funding for career education is an integral part of the implementation process — that it should have been included as a separate topic under that heading. Obviously, adequate funding is a necessary ingredient of something called facilitation. But how is adequate funding to be secured? Who is responsible for securing it? From what sources can it be obtained?

---

*Since these papers were written, Congress enacted Section 406, Title IV, P.L. 93-380, making career education a part of U.S. legislation.

For the reasons implied by the questions, it should be clear that the matter of adequate funding for career education is indeed a serious concern — and that it has major implications for the state education agency. As such, it is treated separately in this chapter, even though the interrelationships noted, as well as others, do exist between funding and implementation.

Career education, as with all aspects of public education, is dependent upon three sources for funding, federal, state, and local. Tax dollars are available only from these sources; there is no question about this. But with the sources as a "given," in what proportion should the necessary funds be made available from the several sources? This is a question for which there is no ready or pat answer, for the "proper" answer will vary from state to state. There is, however, a rule of thumb which might be appropriate for consideration: If the funds are needed for developmental efforts — for seeding purposes — the states might well look to the national level for funds needed to support and facilitate the development or "seeding" process.

Once the development processes have taken place, and if career education is perceived as a legitimate segment of the overall educational program in a state, state education agencies may want to include in the regular educational appropriations — that are proposed — the funds that are needed to maintain career education, including funds for in-service activities.

(In chapter 1, it is emphasized that career education cannot — must not — be perceived as an "add-on" to existing educational programs. Instead, it has been stressed that career education should be an integral part of the existing educational program. This obviously would suggest that considerable support for career education might be found in funds that already are being appropriated in support of education.)

If the funding patterns that have been suggested were to be followed, it would be logical that as career education programs become operational in the schools, the local school systems would assume responsibility for those expenditures normally associated with those agencies — the cost of books, materials, transportation, and so on, related to career education.

The preceding is intended to be suggestive; answers to specific problems and "best procedures" will differ from state to state. The implications for all state education agencies, however, would seem to be quite common to all.

Evaluation

Just as funding is closely related to implementation, so is evaluation closely related to funding. This point has already been made. It is, however, of sufficient import to warrant re-emphasis at this point. The importance of evaluation, in terms of securing adequate funding, is also sufficient to warrant separate treatment of the topic.

Obviously, if career education is — as Hoyt *et al.* (1974) have suggested — a response to a call for reform in American education, and if, as has been suggested by any number of people, career education holds considerable promise in terms of meeting the changing needs of youth and of society, it should be tried. It must be implemented in a carefully planned manner, and it must be implemented with fairly specific goals or purposes in mind. And as it is implemented, provision must be made for determining how well the needs are actually being met, what areas or components are not meeting the needs, and what modifications should be made—to mention but a few. The state education agency, again, is in an ideal position and has an ideal role to facilitate, encourage, and coordinate evaluation efforts.

With the support and leadership of career education personnel in the state education agency, local education agency personnel can develop, or adapt, and administer evaluative instruments that are designed to gather information of the type described earlier. The instruments themselves might well be developed, either in final form or in some adaptive form, by (or under the sponsorship of) state personnel.

Perhaps the key role in evaluation efforts that can be assumed by the state education agency, insofar as career education is concerned, is in the collection, assimilation, analysis, and dissemination of data. As was noted previously, most management information systems do not include provisions for accumulating such data; the implementation process itself has only just begun. But there is a critical need for information about the strengths and weaknesses of career education. Some efforts along these lines are being carried out by the National Institute of Education; others are being encouraged by USOE. Much more will have to be done, however, and the state education agency is, in all probability, the most suitable entity to do the job.

Selected References

Arizona Department of Education. *Career Education: Leadership in Learning*. Phoenix: Arizona Department of Education. 1973.

deBroekert, Carrol; and Kunzman, Leonard. *A Guide for Planning Career Education in Oregon's Secondary Schools*. Salem: Oregon Board of Education. 1970.

DiGuilio, Robert; and Zockle, Michael. "The Teacher Wore a Hardhat." *Career Digest* (December 1973).

Florida State Department of Education. *Career Education in Florida: An Official Department of Education Position Paper*. Tallahassee: Florida State Department of Education. 1973.

Kansas State Department of Education. "Within Reach: Career Education for Every Kansan." Topeka: Kansas State Department of Education. 1973. Mimeographed.

Maryland State Department of Education. "Career Education: Five-Year Action Plan." Baltimore: Maryland State Department of Education. 1972. Mimeographed.

McMinn, J. H.; and Morris, Ken. *Career Education: A Handbook for Program Initiation*. Jackson: Mississippi State Department of Education. 1973.

Morphet, Edgar L.; Jesser, David L.; and Ludka, Arthur P. *Planning and Providing for Excellence in Education*. New York: Citation Press. 1972.

Parnell, Dale; and Kunzman, Leonard. *Career Cluster Facilities Guide*. Salem: Oregon Board of Education. 1973.

Pierce, William. "A Rationale for the Career Education Concept." *American Education* (April 1973).

Rasmussen, Marvin; and Carpenter, Leonard. *A Program of Career Education in the Portland Public Schools*. Portland, Oregon: Portland Public Schools. 1971.

Reich, Charles. *The Greening of America*. New York: Random House, Inc. 1970.

Smith, Russell. *Career Education in Tennessee*. Nashville: Tennessee State Department of Education. 1973.

Texas Education Agency. *Basic Learner Outcomes for Career Education*. Austin: Texas Education Agency. 1973.

United States Senate. *Educational Amendments of 1974: Report, together with supplemental and additional view, of the Committee on Labor and Public Welfare, United States Senate, on S. 1539*. Washington, D.C.: United States Senate, Report No. 93-763. 1974.

Utah State Board of Education. "A Guide for the Implementation of Career Education in a Local Education Agency." Salt Lake City: Utah State Board of Education. 1973. Mimeographed.

Utah State Board of Education. *Career Education: A New Emphasis for Utah Schools*. Salt Lake City: Utah State Board of Education. 1974.

Walsh, Thomas P. *Blueprint for the Possible: A Citizen's Program for Better Schools*. Washington, D.C.: Chamber of Commerce of the United States. 1973.

Afterword

Throughout this book an attempt has been made to focus on career education and the state education agency. It is obvious that the authors believe in the potential of that agency. No other education agency is in a position to attack and solve statewide problems in education; no other agency is in a position to facilitate, support, and maintain needed educational changes — i.e., career education — on a statewide basis.

The authors of this book would in no way imply that the translation of the concept of career education from an idea to a reality will be a simple task. They would, however, strongly suggest that without the leadership, support, and facilitative assistance of the state education agency, it will be an impossible task.

The several roles that might be taken seem to be clear; the implications seem to stand out with equal clarity. What remains, then, is the job itself. Suggestions have been made as to how the job might be accomplished, and models have been used for illustrative purposes. Most of the suggestions and models have been generated by the people who will be and *are* getting the job done. These of course are the state directors and coordinators of career education — the professional educators in the state education agency who are charged with the responsibility for translating a concept into a reality.

Index